Balkan Imbroglio

Balkan Imbroglio

Politics and Security in Southeastern Europe

Daniel N. Nelson

Routledge
Taylor & Francis Group
NEW YORK AND LONDON

First published in 1991 by Westview Press

Published in 2021 by Routledge
605 Third Avenue, New York, NY 10017
2 Park Square, Milton Park, Abingdon, Oxon OX14 4RN

Routledge is an imprint of the Taylor & Francis Group, an informa business

Copyright © 1991 by Taylor & Francis

All rights reserved. No part of this book may be reprinted or reproduced or utilised in any form or by any electronic, mechanical, or other means, now known or hereafter invented, including photocopying and recording, or in any information storage or retrieval system, without permission in writing from the publishers.

Notice:
Product or corporate names may be trademarks or registered trademarks, and are used only for identification and explanation without intent to infringe.

Library of Congress Cataloging-in-Publication Data
Nelson, Daniel N., 1948–
   Balkan imbroglio : politics and security in southeastern Europe /
Daniel N. Nelson.
      p.   cm.
   Includes index.
   ISBN 0-8133-7956-3
   1. Balkan Peninsula—Politics and government—1989–   . 2. Balkan
Peninsula—Foreign relations—1989–   . I. Title.
DR48.6.N45   1991
949.6—dc20   90-29096
                                                                          CIP

ISBN 13: 978-0-3670-1482-7 (hbk)
ISBN 13: 978-0-3671-6469-0 (pbk)

Contents

Preface   vii

Introduction   1

Notes, 6

1 Security in the Balkans   7

Multilateral Effects on Balkan Domestic Politics
  and Foreign Policies, 9
The Soviet Union and Southeastern Europe, 23
Military Doctrine, 24
Regional Security Issues, 26
Conclusion, 27
Notes, 29

2 The Yugoslav Precipice   35

Federalism to Confederalism to Nationalism, 35
Economic Paralysis, 40
Potent Nationalism, 43
Yugoslav Strengths, 47
Implications for Western Policy, 49
Notes, 52

3 New Politics and the Army in Bulgaria   55

Propellants of Change, 55
The Army and Bulgaria's Transitions, 66
Notes, 70

**4 No Longer Tyranny, Not Yet Democracy:
Romania's Perilous Path After Ceausescu**   75

Background, 75
Electoral Outcomes, 82

v

Post-Electoral Unrest and Western Responses, 85
Conclusion, 88
Notes, 88

**5 Turkish Uncertainties: Domestic and Foreign
Policy Identities in the 1990s**   91

Introduction, 91
Domestic Policies, 91
Turkey and Strategic Realignment, 95
Notes, 105

6 Athenian Questions   109

The Political and Economic Quagmire, 109
Greek Foreign Policy Adjustments, 113
Summary, 116
Notes, 116

Conclusion: Balkan Pasts, Balkan Futures   119

Balkan Futures, 121
Notes, 123

Index   125

Preface

As Europe underwent extraordinary changes in 1989–1990, the continent's southeastern region—the Balkans—began once again to distinguish itself through ethnic rivalries, political turmoil, and interstate disputes. The recurrence of tensions and conflicts between age-old antagonists and an uncertain prognosis for stability, democracy, and well-being have fostered images of a "Balkan imbroglio" where there is little hope of progress and ample reason to suspect worse. From the outside the Balkans do, indeed, convey a sense of political intricacies and confusions that entangle anyone who ventures near.

This volume offers country-specific and comparative assessments of principal political trends during such a transitional era. The contents were written in the midst of significant regional and indigenous changes and reflect the dynamism of the period. I have made no effort to survey the entire range of events from Yugoslav to Turkish politics, but concentrate instead on matters of international security, socioeconomic policy, and political leadership. I focus, in other words, on the most visible part of the political spectrum during this turbulent era, anticipating that readers will pursue additional sources for detailed consideration of nuances in each country's domestic scene. Although I have been drawn toward the unfolding of events in 1989–1990, I am concerned as well about theoretical issues—about the requisite conditions for democracy, the role of the military in a civil society, and the manner in which security can be achieved other than from an overarching multilateral alliance.

I have been aided in the production of this book by the staff at the Carnegie Endowment for International Peace, where I was a senior associate during 1990. Liz Jasper was an exceptionally able administrative assistant, and Tom Perc, Jackie Merl, Julie Baumgarten, and Andy Howard served as researchers on various aspects of this project.

Chapter 1 is reprinted with the permission of the Woodrow Wilson International Center for Scholars from Paul S. Shoup, ed., and George W. Hoffman, project director, *Problems of Balkan Security: Southeastern Europe in the 1990s* (Washington, D.C.: Wilson Center Press, 1990), pp. 123–150. Copyright 1990 by the Woodrow Wilson International Center for Scholars. Chapter 2 updates an article that was in *Revue d'études viii* *Preface*

comparatives Est-Ouest, vol. 21, no. 4 (Fall 1990). Chapter 3 is a revised version of a report for the Bundesinstitut für Ostwissenschaftliche und Internationale Studien, 32-1990. Chapter 4 was published initially in *Electoral Studies,* vol. 9, no. 4 (Fall 1990). A version of Chapter 5 first appeared in the Spring 1990 (#19) issue of *The National Interest,* Washington, D.C.

Daniel N. Nelson
Washington, D.C.

Introduction

"The Balkans" is a term connoting peoples, cultures and states that make up a peninsula of Southeastern Europe between the Black, Adriatic, Aegean and Mediterranean seas. The Balkan Mountains are at the heart of this region, running a few hundred miles from eastern Yugoslavia through Bulgaria. To the north and northwest, however, the boundary of the Balkans is less precise, and loudly debated.

During the latter half of the twentieth century, the post–World War II boundaries of Romania and Yugoslavia have been taken as the northern extent of the Balkan region. The Austro-Hungarian Empire, of course, earlier had controlled Slovenia and Croatia (since 1918, republics of Yugoslavia), as well as Transylvania (within Romania today), making their "Balkan" character questionable in some ethnographic and geographic studies.

In this volume, however, I adopt a pragmatic definition, using the boundaries of the Yugoslav and Romanian states after World War II as the northern division of the Balkans from the rest of Europe, and also include the European salient of Turkey to the west of the Bosporus.

"The Balkans" inspire disparaging assessments, visions of backwardness, corruption and intrigue, or (in the popular mind) Dracula and the Orient Express. Behind this facade, however, are nations and states exhibiting more substance and complexity, more capacity and depth. Thorough, scholarly histories of the Balkans reveal periods of peace and development during the past century that, had they been able to continue unimpeded, may have led to a far different environment than today's conditions. Unfortunately for the populations of the region, the emphasis of Balkan governments after gaining independence from the Turks and Austro-Hungarian Empire was on ". . . military preparedness and national expansion over internal development . . ." while ". . . fail[ing] to pay adequate attention to the concerns and interests of the peasantry or to give adequate support to the agricultural sections of their economies."[1]

1

The human and natural resources of the region, however, could have created a different outcome.

The Balkans deserve our attention. Often in the recent past this region has been the locus of events that triggered conflagrations throughout Europe and the world. Warfare in the region was begun as Balkan nations sought to shake off Ottoman Turk domination in the nineteenth century. The revolts of 1877 elicited Russian intervention against the Turks. After Alexander II's forces secured an Ottoman defeat and an independent Bulgaria in the Treaty of San Stefano, raising fears of Russian hegemony in Southeastern Europe, other European powers intervened to demand that another treaty (the Treaty of Berlin) return much of Bulgaria to the Turks.

Further Balkan warfare in 1912–1913 involved defeat for the Turks by an alliance of nations, and then Bulgaria's defeat when it sought to extend its territory in Macedonia and Thrace. And, of course, it was the assassination of Austrian Archduke Ferdinand in Sarajevo in 1914 that began the chain of mobilization and war preparations which led resolutely towards combat in August of that year.

Between the World Wars, the Balkans never found any breathing space, with military coups, royal dictatorships, fascist and communist agitation, all contributing to two decades of considerable difficulty. The sovereignty that the states had gained from Austro-Hungary and the Turks did not ensure their political quiescence or international security; underdeveloped and without self-governing experience, they were ripe for domination by larger European powers and for destabilization by extremist ideologies.

Once again, in the 1990s, we find the Balkans to have regained a sense of autonomy as the strategic retreat of the Soviet Union continues apace and American concerns are directed elsewhere. But there is little assurance of peace and prosperity in Southeastern Europe. Festering for decades, and now once again out in the open, deeply embedded ethnic rivalries and territorial disputes are buffeting each political system. Whether or not these resurgent issues will have the same disruptive and disastrous consequences as at other times in the last century is uncertain. But we *can* be sure that a smooth transition towards developed and stable civil societies will be made far more difficult by these indigenous conditions. We can also be sure that the larger picture of European integration and security will be troubled by the Balkan imbroglio, with hopes and plans for the continent's economic and political union always confronting the vicissitudes of its southeastern peninsula.

The Balkans deserve our attention, too, because these states and nations retain the distinction of being a meeting ground for Europe and Asia as much as, if not more so than, the Urals. In Southeastern Europe, Islam and Christian Europe intermingle, and within the Christian faiths

Introduction 3

are also Orthodoxy, Catholicism and Protestantism. Cultural and religious lines are blurred; Turks, of course, are Moslems, as are most Albanians. Yet Islam is also present among perhaps 15% of Bulgarian citizens (including Turks and Bulgarian Moslems known as Pomaks) and a similar proportion of the Yugoslav population concentrated in southern republics. Orthodox Christianity is strongest in Romania, Bulgaria, Serbia and Greece, but retains a symbolic presence in Turkey (most obviously in Istanbul). Protestant sects are active in Transylvania, Slovenia, and Croatia, but particularly in the latter two one finds Roman Catholicism to be dominant.[2] Although all of Europe became more "plural" due to immigration during the 1970s and 1980s, the Balkans remain the region of greatest diversity, wherein cultural, linguistic and ethnic combinations are most complex. The heterogeneity of the six states of the region varies, but all exhibit the components of volatility which can erupt once again into larger conflicts.[3]

We should also be aware of demographic trends that already portend significant political dilemmas. Albanians and Turks were, during the 1980s, the fastest growing ethnic groups in Europe; the Albanian growth rate, for the population within the Albanian state, exceeded 3% annually, while the population of Turkey grew at an annual rate averaging 2.4% in the 1980s.[4] Albanians within the Yugoslav republic of Serbia, concentrated in the Kosovo region where they constitute 90% of the population, have raised demands for autonomy which have been resisted and turned into a Serbian nationalist issue by Slobodan Milosevic. Turks within Bulgaria likewise have a very high birthrate, altering over time the ethnic composition of the Bulgarian state. There, too, the communist and post-communist governments have confronted in very different ways the challenge of ethnic heterogeneity.

With the population growth of Turks and Albanians, the Balkan states (including all of Turkey) will exceed 130 million by 1995.[5] The European Community (EC) already grapples with politically troublesome issues of economic migration from East-Central and Southeastern Europe (plus, in France and Italy, an influx of North Africans). With a combined population of more than half that of the EC, however, and economies severely retarded by underdevelopment and/or years of state ownership and central planning, the potential for a mass exodus to more advanced and prosperous states suggests unsettling choices for Western Europe in the 1990s and beyond.

Balkan poverty is also an issue that compels our attention. Not only by European standards, but increasingly by world standards, there are parts of Southeastern Europe that are *very* poor. Aggregate statistics of per capita income and consumption levels do not tell the story. These data are skewed by much better conditions in parts of larger federal states (e.g., the northern republic of Slovenia is far better off than Macedonia, Montenegro or parts of Serbia, and the districts inhabited by Turks in Bulgaria have far lower per capita measures of wealth) or in capital cities (if we compare, for example, Athens with the remote north of Greece or Bucharest with the desperately poor rural areas and small cities in outlying counties).[6]

Accelerating economic crises of the 1980s in Eastern Europe, particularly in the latter half of the decade, no doubt contributed to the events of 1989–1990. A report by the Joint Economic Committe of the U.S. Congress in 1989, for example, pointed to a general decline in Eastern Europe's economic performance, with Bulgaria and Romania suffering particularly precipitous drops in the 1986 to 1989 period. John Hardt and Richard Kaufman noted that "[s]tandards of living . . . are on the thin margin of acceptability or worse, and have stagnated or fallen throughout Eastern Europe in the 1980s."[7] Simultaneously, Greek and Turkish inflation was skyrocketing (the Turkish level reached over 70% annually by 1988–1989) and debt was growing rapidly; unlike East European communist states of the 1980s, Greece and Turkey did not have stagnant economies, but instead exhibited uncontrolled government-driven growth that exacerbated inequalities. Most Turks shared little in the prosperity of Istanbul and the coast, while northern Greece remained poverty stricken throughout the economic expansion fueled by EC membership.

Perhaps the most critical matter that demands our attention to the Balkans is the struggle for democratic values and institutions that is now underway. In Greece and Turkey, this confrontation between authoritarianism and the rule of law is not new, and certainly predates the collapse of communist regimes in most of Europe during 1989–1990. Post–World War II generations in both states have had to confront the threat of left-wing revolution and/or terrorism *and* right-wing military juntas. Greek politics have traversed a civil war, monarchy, a reactionary army dictatorship, and a turbulent swing from left-wing socialists and conservatives. There has been little time for stable democratic institutions to develop unimpeded in Greece. Turkey, of course, has seen military coups in 1960 and 1980, between which was a period of virulent internal violence. Simultaneously, Kurdish separatists and other groups mount attacks against military and police, plus transport, communications and other facilities in the eastern portions of the country.

The other four Balkan states, for four decades under communist rule, now exhibit considerable diversity. Still holding on, but clearly unstable, is the communist regime in Tirana, led by Ramiz Alia. Only by establishing a military and police cordon around most Western embassies in Tirana did the Alia regime bring a temporary halt to a large flow of citizens into the compounds of those legations, demanding asylum. Several

Introduction

thousand, in fact, were flown out of Albania by Western governments in early 1990, after having occupied embassy compounds. This, obviously, is the tip of a much larger iceberg that suggests impending turmoil within Albania.

In Romania and Bulgaria, "communist" governments no longer exist, although parties that consist of erstwhile communists did win contested elections in May and June, respectively. Todor Zhivkov's ouster in November 1989, and Nicolae Ceausescu's demise and execution in late December, meant the end of one-party control. In neither of these states, however, has the political culture made the transition to the plural, competitive, civil society in which democracy ideally functions. They will not soon make it to that point, although one party dictatorship has been defeated. Tenets of open, tolerant political life, guided by the rule of law, are as of yet far from being firmly in place. Miners are called in to defend an elected government from angry protesters while the Army and police stand by; Romania's transition away from tyranny has a rough road ahead. Meanwhile, the Bulgarian Socialist Party (that consists of many who were moderates and reformers in the old Bulgarian Communist Party) headquarters is set ablaze in Sofia, as police respond slowly. These events of summer 1990 are palpable examples of the many obstacles remaining towards anything resembling a working democracy as these Balkan societies go through the wrenching process of ridding themselves of communist vestiges—central planning, the nomenklatura, and the secret police.

Meanwhile, in Yugoslavia, the existence of the state is at issue in the 1990s. Changes towards multiparty elections, free press, and private ownership have been effected to a substantial degree already in Slovenia and Croatia. Far less movement is evident in the largest of Yugoslavia's republics, Serbia. And, as the northern republics advance steadily towards a more plural and open political and socioeconomic environment, while Serbia, Montenegro, Macedonia and Bosnia-Hercogovina are more constrained by older ideas, the ethnic rivalries and suspicions are exacerbated, and the potential for violent conflict rises further.

This reading of Balkan issues is stark. The most populous, demographically fastest growing and poorest region of Europe is, simultaneously, its most volatile. To any observer, these characteristics spell trouble.

In the following chapters, I explore principal domestic, regional and international dynamics affecting the Balkan's prognoses for the 1990s and beyond. Implicit to my consideration of the region and each country is an underlying question to which I will return in my concluding essay, i.e., what are the chances that the peoples and states of the Balkans *can*, indeed, arrive at a stable, secure and prosperous future?

Notes

1. Barbara Jelavich, *History of the Balkans* Volume 2 (New York: Cambridge University Press, 1983), p. 3.

2. One of the few efforts to estimate religious affiliation, a datum not gathered in the census calculations of communist party governments, was Ivan Volgyes, *Politics in Eastern Europe* (Chicago: Dorsey, 1986), p. 207.

3. An empirical examination of heterogeneity throughout Eastern Europe was the subject of my paper "Security and Society in Eastern Europe: A Research Note" (Washington, D.C.: Carnegie Endowment, unpublished manuscript).

4. Author's calculations based on data from the Central Intelligence Agency's *Handbook of Economic Statistics, 1988* (Washington, D.C.: CIA, Directorate of Intelligence, 1988), p. 46–47.

5. Author's calculations projecting average annual growth rates of the 1980s into the 1990s, based on data in Ibid.

6. Regional inequalities, particularly as they affected the communist states in the region during the 1970s and 1980s, were discussed in detail in portions of Daniel N. Nelson, ed., *Communism and the Politics of Inequalities* (Lexington, Mass.: Lexington Books, 1983).

7. John P. Hardt and Richard F. Kaufman, "Introduction" in Joint Economic Committee, U.S. Congress, *Pressures for Reform in the East European Economies,* Volume 1 (Washington, D.C.: Government Printing Office, October 20, 1989), p. x.

1

Security in the Balkans

Principal conflicts of Southeastern Europe and its Balkan core have not been denoted by post-war East-West alliances. Conflicts embedded in Southeastern Europe predate by centuries the two international treaty organizations NATO (1949) and the Warsaw Pact* (1955). In the Pact, the Hungarian-Romanian dispute over Romanian treatment of ethnic Hungarians in Transylvania has been resurgent. Enmity between Greece and Turkey, nominal allies within the context of NATO, is rooted in ancient territorial arguments, the Cyprus stalemate, and other issues.

Even between members of the opposing alliances, disputes have had little to do with the East-West confrontation. Bulgarian treatment of Turkish nationals brought Ankara and Sofia to a point of severe acrimony, for example, and no one invoked NATO and the Warsaw Pact.

The Soviets no doubt saw the Warsaw Pact as a symbol of their determination to retain Eastern Europe in their grasp.[1] Yet, in 1955, when the Pact was founded, no senior Soviet officer would have thought of East European armies as adjuncts to Soviet offensive capabilities against NATO; they were poorly equipped and lacked any training with Soviet forces, and Warsaw Pact structures were largely inactive until the early 1960s.[2] The inauguration of joint exercises in 1961 began to change the character of the Warsaw Pact, but did not rapidly transform East European armies into instruments for offensive operations against NATO.

Simply put, the Soviet intention was to use the Warsaw Pact to impose a superpower perspective on Eastern Europe's security. Ideally, Moscow sought a tightly knit, compliant, impermeable alliance characterized by high levels of intraalliance foreign-policy agreement; high responsiveness to Soviet signals and examples; and resistance to Western, Chinese, or

---

*Formally, the Warsaw Treaty Organization or WTO.

other overtures. Had the USSR been entirely successful in that goal, three original southeast European Warsaw Pact members—Bulgaria, Romania, and (until 1968) Albania—would have adopted security policies highly consistent with one another and with Moscow, and nationalistic issues would have faded in importance.

But the Soviets failed. East European members of the Warsaw Pact, particularly those of Southeastern Europe, never understood their security in ways consistent with the USSR or each other. They did not respond uniformly to Soviet signals or examples, and all flirted with powers that, at various times, Moscow saw as threatening long before Soviet hegemony came unglued in 1989.

Important questions arise from such general observations. If the Soviets did not succeed in imbuing East European Communist Party regimes or peoples with a collective view (that is, a Soviet view) of security, how was that failure evident in multilateral or bilateral relations and the alliance behavior of non-Soviet Warsaw Pact (NSWP) members in Southeastern Europe—that is, Romania and Bulgaria? Conversely, in what sense was the Warsaw Pact instrumental in enforcing behavior among those Soviet allies consistent with collective security, notwithstanding perceptions of indigenous elites or masses?

Outside the Warsaw Pact, but with governing Communist parties, issues also arise about the effects of the Warsaw Pact on Yugoslavia and Albania. For Yugoslavia, the political-military implications of a hostile international treaty organization were ominous. For the first decade of the Warsaw Pact, the military contribution of NSWP states in Southeastern Europe to any threat Moscow wished to mount against Tito was small, and the Pact therefore changed little from the standpoint of Yugoslav military planning. Yet when NSWP forces participated in the invasion of Czechoslovakia of August 1968, the military implications of the Warsaw Pact were heightened. For Albania, despite the ideological break of 1961, Tirana did not withdraw from the Warsaw Pact until 1968, and Hoxha's involvement with China reflected the political and military danger implicit in a departure from the collective fold of the Warsaw Pact.

My focus here is on erstwhile communist states of Southeastern Europe, Romania and Bulgaria, and on those where communist parties still play important roles—Yugoslavia and Albania. Both Greece and Turkey will be noted in terms of their relations with one or more of these states. The discussion is divided into two parts: first, the effects of multinational treaty organizations on domestic politics and international policies of states in the region and, second, the military doctrine of, and principal security issues confronting each country.

Multilateral Effects on Balkan Domestic Politics
and Foreign Policies

Romania

Nicolae Ceausescu, in the first decade of his quarter-century in power, used the Warsaw Pact and the USSR artfully as threats against which to rally domestic support. These threats were, of course, not entirely figments of Ceausescu's political imagination. Indeed, in late 1968 and again in the early 1970s, there was cause for Romanian concern that a Soviet-led Warsaw Pact intervention would be mounted.[3]

The high-water mark of Ceausescu's domestic mass legitimacy came at an August 1968 rally in Bucharest, when he called for the defense of the homeland against those who posed an imminent threat. Romania's condemnation of the invasion of Czechoslovakia, close relations with Mao's China, and other behavior had incurred Brezhnev's wrath, and there were signs of preparations for an invasion.[4] Anti-Russian sentiment, historically strong in the old Romanian provinces of Wallachia and Moldavia, was heightened by Soviet occupation after World War II and the stationing of the Red Army in Romania until 1958. To these long-standing suspicions of Russian intentions was added, with vivid clarity because of the Czechoslovak invasion, antipathy toward the Warsaw Pact's role as an enforcer of Soviet hegemony and the role that might be played by two NSWP neighbors, Hungary and Bulgaria, in aiding the USSR in "multilateral" action against Romania.

The short-term effect of military action to enforce the Brezhnev Doctrine—the notion of limited sovereignty within the European "socialist commonwealth"—was to bolster the popular appeal of the regime of a then-young Balkan ruler. Ceausescu was able to accelerate the replacement of party elites who, as elements of a Gheorghiu-Dej cohort, had dubious loyalty to Ceausescu.[5] He was also able, for a few years at least, to pose as the benefactor of ethnic tolerance and cooperation, government reform, and intellectual and artistic liberalization.

In fact, of course, Ceausescu in 1968 was merely tapping a Romanian-Russian enmity that had, only two-and-a-half decades earlier, led to willing Romanian participation in the German invasion of the USSR.[6] Beginning in 1971, the legitimacy Ceausescu had been able to garner in 1968 began to dissipate. Ceausescu's true intentions became evident as an ideological crackdown was imposed in 1971 and intellectual freedom was rolled back over the next few years. And, as has been told elsewhere, the excesses of a cult of personality—first for Nicolae Ceausescu, and later for his wife, Elena, and extended family—began to consume the Romanian political landscape.[7]

Ceausescu never gave up his efforts to use the Warsaw Pact as a *cause célèbre*. A decade after the Warsaw Pact invasion of Czechoslovakia, Ceausescu abruptly returned from meetings of Communist Party leaders from all seven Pact members in the Soviet Union to announce that Romania would not accede to Soviet insistence that all Warsaw Pact members raise military spending levels and pursue similar policies in out-of-area issues (such as the Middle East). In this instance, Ceausescu's lieutenants organized mass rallies in Bucharest to replicate in size, if not spirit, the 1968 event.[8]

By the late 1980s, however, Ceausescu's appeals, although still audible, were overtaken by events. The advent of Mikhail Gorbachev placed Ceausescu in the awkward position of trying to defend an "independent course" vis-à-vis Moscow that rejected reform, moderation, and pragmatism, while causing untold suffering for the Romanian population.

Ironically, even before Gorbachev, the path of a sometimes noncompliant member of the Warsaw Pact did not have uniformly positive political consequences. The domestic requirements of playing a disjunctive role in the Warsaw Pact included devoting a substantial social and economic effort to the foolhardy goal of near-autarky in the economy. Although he maintained very high levels of investment (30 to 35% of national income) over long periods of time, Ceausescu's notion of *dezvoltare multilateral* never connoted much in the way of higher living standards for Romanians.[9] Instead, less and less efficient industry was created in the Stalinist mode of extensive growth, yielding huge enterprises that produced large quantities of unmarketable materials. When these policies yielded the inevitable economic disaster, Ceausescu could not turn to the Soviets or to the West for assistance, and so he imposed a policy of austerity that continued until his demise. It is small wonder that Ceausescu's regime suffered a massive turnaround in levels of public support and ruled in its last years the most disaffected population in Communist Europe.[10]

At the same time, a military doctrine that reduced the role of the professional army in national defense led to strained civil-military relations. This strain became a political issue because of the interdependence of the army and party. Neither could keep its authority without the aid of the other, and each distrusted the other's intentions.

Signs of this disenchantment were imprecise, but suggestive nonetheless. There was, for example, the case of General Ion Serb who was arrested in early 1972, for passing details of China's ties with Romania to the USSR's military attache in Bucharest. Because this arrest was followed by a number of high-ranking personnel changes in the army high command

Security in the Balkans

and in the Ministry of Internal Affairs, some analysts speculated about ties to a coup attempt.[11] Although other analysts doubted these tenuous linkages,[12] Ceausescu certainly was not confident about his relationship with the army's officer corps during the early 1970s.

A decade later, Ceausescu could no longer be assured of the military's support. Because of Romania's desperate economic straits in 1982, the Romanian leader announced at a December 1982 party conference that military expenditures would be frozen at the 1982 level until 1985.[13] Although the announcement was couched in rhetoric about arms reductions, the officer corps was certainly not deceived. Once again, rumors of a military coup reached the West in early 1983—rumors that were made more credible by their coincidence with Ceausescu's attempt to squeeze the military budget further and by the evident failure of that attempt. In both those years, expenditure and manpower increases were apparent.[14]

By the end of 1985, Ceausescu was forced to admit that the army was plagued with dissatisfaction. His reassignment of Colonel General Constantin Olteanu from defense minister to head of the Bucharest party organization in early 1986 was a careful move, consistent with his long-standing policy to rotate cadres among posts. While avoiding any clear demotion of Olteanu (who later also lost that position), Ceausescu sought to constrain the political voice of the army. For lower-ranking officers other tools were used in the effort to limit political challenges—intensive ideological training and the overlapping sources of authority available to Ceausescu through the Romanian Communist Party, the state, and the Defense Council (of which he was the chairman).

Out of necessity, Ceausescu tried to placate the Romanian army as he encountered more and more mass hostility. This effort to repair fences with the military was implied by the inverse trends of public support and defense expenditures in Romania.[15] Isolated from Soviet support in the Gorbachev period, and politically distant from the West because of a sordid human-rights record and undependable economic ventures, Ceausescu fell back on the military and secret police as his defense from the people he ruled.

The elevations of Mikhail Gorbachev to the post of General Secretary of the Communist Party of the Soviet Union (CPSU) propelled Ceausescu much further away from the Soviets than ever before.[16] Ceausescu repeatedly denied the compatibility of socialism and economic decentralization or political pluralism. Indeed, only hours before the former Soviet President Andrei Gromyko arrived in Bucharest in May 1988, Ceausescu went so far as to warn against "rightist deviation" as the "principal danger" to socialism.[17] From the perspective of other Warsaw Pact members, Romania's exacerbation of tension with Hungary over ethnic Hungarians in Transylvania was perhaps the most dangerous aspect of Ceausescu's relations within the Pact. The exodus of ethnic Hungarians from Romania during 1988 alone exceeded 12,000. The presence of *refugees* escaping from one Warsaw Pact member into another created "an explosive political problem" within the Soviet-led alliance, which became worse as Ceausescu started to go ahead with his plan to raze thousands of villages throughout the country (thereby doing grievous harm to minority languages and cultures that survive only in the countryside), with populations moved into new "agroindustrial centers."[18]

Whereas once criticism of the Soviet Union and the Warsaw Pact served to raise Ceausescu's stature, the utility of attacking the Pact for this purpose had faded. By the late 1980s, continued emphasis on going it alone meant staying aloof from processes of change and reform, not the assertion of national independence from the USSR. Pact members began to view Ceausescu not merely as a deviant of nationalist bent, but as a palpable danger to the region's peace and stability. Political costs from Ceausescu's adamant rejection of socioeconomic moderation could no longer be avoided by referring to implicit Warsaw Pact threats and limitations on Romanian sovereignty. Not only did the Romanian public abandon its *Conducatorul;* even the Romanian army set its sights on a post-Ceausescu era.[19]

Bulgaria

For Todor Zhivkov's Bulgaria, membership in the Warsaw Pact was a politically comfortable, albeit socioeconomically burdensome, association. Zhivkov led the Bulgarian Communist Party (BCP) for the first three-and-a-half decades of Warsaw Pact history. Fealty to the USSR—demonstrated through thorough political, economic, and military integration via both the Pact and the Council for Mutual Economic Assistance (CMEA)—was the hallmark of Zhivkov's foreign and security policies.

Unlike Ceausescu, Zhivkov's regime never sought to maintain, or even to discuss, a war-fighting capability distinct from Bulgaria's role in the Combined Armed Forces of the Warsaw Pact. The idea of a territorial defense as undertaken by Yugoslavia and Romania was an anathema to Sofia. The BCP leaders consistently directed a higher proportion of the country's gross national product (GNP) to military spending than any other NSWP state, and maintained the highest military manpower levels as a proportion of population among all Warsaw Pact members except the USSR.[20]

The country's militarization within the Warsaw Pact meant that, notwithstanding Bulgaria's rising living standards relative to the USSR (Bulgaria had Eastern Europe's most quickly rising net material product—

Security in the Balkans 13

NMP—per capita from 1965 through 1981), very little of Bulgaria's economic growth was controlled by Bulgarians.[21]

Bulgaria has depended on the USSR and other East European Warsaw Pact members for more than ¾ of all imports and exports, 57% of which were (at the end of the 1980s) to and from the Soviet Union. As the least energy self-sufficient of all NSWP states, Bulgaria imports seventy percent of its oil and natural gas from the USSR.[22] The net effect of this profound economic dependency was to limit drastically Bulgaria's freedom to make decisions that might damage Soviet security interests. Indeed, Bulgarian discussions of this matter acknowledged in the Zhivkov period that "full coordination [and] intensified . . . economic and military-economic integration [with the] entire socialist community and, above all [with] the Soviet Union" were vital.[23] It is quite clear that Bulgaria's defense expenditures, and entire defense industry, were adjuncts of Soviet security interests in the guise of coalitional Warsaw Pact efforts.

Political effects of security policies on Zhivkov's regime were less clear. Zhivkov and his defense minister, Dobri Dzhurov, continued to justify the heavy commitments to the Bulgarian armed forces on the basis of ties to the Soviet Union and to the defense of socialism. But there was little in those justifications that could rationalize the level of effort, which fell in the highest decile of all nation-states regarding military force levels per 1,000 population, and between the 80th and 90th percentile for military expenditures as a proportion of GNP.[24]

Socioeconomic costs of Bulgarian military effort on behalf of the Soviets and the Warsaw Pact were imprecise but tangible. Yet it is important to note the weaknesses in critical elements of the Bulgarian economic infrastructure. In transport, for example, Bulgaria has far less rail capacity than either Romania or Hungary, and its civilian airline is merely symbolic.[25] Moreover, the failure to develop alternatives to the Soviet Union in foreign trade left Bulgaria extraordinarily isolated from the world economy in the aftermath of 1989–1990 political changes, notwithstanding the country's relatively high level of industrialization.

Subservience to the Soviet Union also led to tensions within the military. Although the history of party-army relations in Bulgaria has received more detailed comments elsewhere,[26] we should recount here that the Red Army never took the Bulgarian Army's obeisance to Soviet dominance for granted. Even as the Bulgarian army changed sides in the closing months of World War II, Bulgarian-born political commissars who had served in the Red Army and Soviet "training officers" began infiltrating the army's ranks.[27] At the same time, Red Army divisions bracketed the Bulgarian units.[28] Once the war had ended, the Soviets used this control over the Bulgarian army to reshape it into a "Bulgarian People's Army" (BPA).

Soviet control over the BPA apparently was not strong enough to overcome resentment in the army toward Bulgaria's subservient status. In 1961 rumors of a plot against Zhivkov spread to the West, but the coup attempt could never be corroborated.[29]

More solid evidence exists of a planned coup attempt in 1965. Early in that year, apparently prompted by the ouster of Nikita Khrushchev in October 1964, the commander of the Sofia garrison, General Tsviatko Anev, along with Todorov-Gorunia (a Bulgarian Central Committee member) and several others, planned to seize key party and state offices, as well as major transportation and communication centers, and to topple the Zhivkov regime. Although further details are sketchy, we know that the conspirators were discovered, arrested, and imprisoned before they had the opportunity to take any military action. Several years later, various BCP investigations indicated that the conspiracy had penetrated deeply into district party committees and into other military commands.[30]

We do not know precisely what led to the coup attempt, but there are grounds for informed speculation. First, the 1961 plot was rumored to have involved a core of top BPA officers who had served together as anti-Nazi Partisans in World War II. The Partisans, unlike the Communist Bulgarians who served with the Red Army, had fought to oust the Germans before a Soviet invasion. After the war the Partisan officers no doubt retained their allegiance to the Bulgarian nation and people. Several of the 1965 conspirators had also been Partisans, and the timing of the plot following Khrushchev's removal in the Soviet Union suggests a desire for greater autonomy on the part of Bulgaria in its relationship with the USSR at a time that leadership difficulties in Moscow provided an opportunity for distancing Sofia from the Soviet Union. Finally, there were indications in 1960 that BPA commanders were worried about their uncertain political control of the army and concerned about failures to abide by "the Party line in the army."[31] More than two and a half decades later, a new Bulgarian leadership remains nervous about the army's loyalty. Military leaders continually emphasize in the army's principal organ, *Narodna Armiya*, BPA loyalty and esprit.[32]

To these ongoing concerns about the army must be added the issue of ethnic mistrust and national conflict, which escalated in the 1980s into open hostility and violence. Ethnic Turks and Bulgarian Moslems (Pomaks) together constituted as of early 1989, 12–15% of Bulgaria's population, depending on whose estimate is used. Their birthrate is substantially higher than the rate for the Bulgarian majority, and the gradual enlargement of these minorities would have been expected had the expulsion and large-scale emigration of April–September, 1989, not taken place. During those few months, perhaps 300,000 Turks fled to Turkey, many expelled and others fearing reprisals after ethnic protests.

Security in the Balkans 15

(Even so, many Turks returned later and the net loss in population was perhaps 200,000.)

In 1983–1985, ethnic violence flared in many towns and border *okrugs* (districts) where one part of the Turkish population is concentrated. The protests were directed against Zhivkov's policies to end Turkish-language publications and educational programs, and to require Bulgarian surnames of all Bulgarian citizens.[33] Turkish sources reported more than 1,000 deaths.[34] In 1989, the situation once again exploded, as Turkish protest led to police and army crackdowns, followed by mass expulsions. It is apparent, in this connection, that the Turkish population in Bulgaria would be a great liability to Bulgaria in time of war, especially if the BPA engaged the Turkish army. More immediately, the ethnic unrest raises problems concerning the conscription of ethnic Turks into the BPA, and the possibility that the BPA will be permanently involved in ensuring domestic order in regions of the country inhabited by the Turkish minority.

Before 1985, Sofia's international involvement consisted almost entirely of economic, political, and military associations with other Warsaw Pact members *or* of economic and military aid to Soviet clients in the Third World. Indeed, as late as 1986 less than $\frac{1}{20}$ of all Bulgarian trade was with Turkey, Greece, Yugoslavia, Albania, and Romania.[35]

Held in check by Soviet interests and Warsaw Pact integration, Bulgaria was, in the 1970s through mid-1980s, a reluctant and cautious participant in Balkan diplomatic interaction. In the January 1976 Balkan Conference, Sofia's involvement was tentative and suspicious. Zhivkov began to explore avenues of bridge building with Western Europe in the early 1980s, but a planned visit to Bonn in 1984 was cancelled in response to Soviet pressures.

The latitude for Bulgarian foreign policy widened somewhat after 1985. The severe strains on Bulgarian-Turkish relations brought on by the nationalities policies described earlier, which became even worse in spring and summer 1989, no doubt contributed to the Zhivkov regime's improving relations with Greece. In September 1986, Bulgaria signed a protocol of friendship with the Papandreou government. The protocol committed Greece and Bulgaria to help each other combat "agitation"— that is ethnic unrest among Turks or Moslems in Bulgaria and Greece or among Macedonian nationalists in both Bulgaria and Greece. Furthermore, the Bulgarian regime tolerated, and perhaps encouraged, environmental protests in Ruse against pollutants emitted from heavy industry in the Romanian city of Giurgiu, suggesting that Sofia was reassessing its relations with Romania. In February 1988, after some initial caution, Bulgaria participated in the Balkan foreign ministers' conference. At the meeting, Bulgarian positions evinced further movement away from strict isolation within the Warsaw Pact, without signaling any basic changes in Bulgarian foreign policy.[36] After the forced resignation of Zhivkov in November, 1989, and a rapid renewal of Bulgarian contacts with Greece as a country sharing common adversaries in both Turkey *and* Macedonia, it is clear that Sofia has wide latitude in how it will pursue security.

There are, then, signs that Bulgaria's foreign policy has become more flexible in recent years, with interests germane to Bulgaria and neighboring states beginning to reassert themselves. As long as Zhivkov was in power, Bulgarian foreign policy nevertheless was guided by support of Warsaw Pact integration and close collaboration with the Soviet Union. After Zhivkov, Bulgaria has begun to cast about for security reinforcements, but will be the last to split decisively from the USSR.

Yugoslavia

When the Warsaw Pact was created by the Soviet Union in May 1955, it meant little for the military situation confronting Tito and Yugoslav communism. Although non-Soviet armies in the new Pact were not imposing at that time, Tito well understood the evident willingness of Moscow to use tanks to crush uprisings (as in East Germany in 1953).

Politically, however, the good news of 1955—the Soviet agreement to withdraw from Austria and the overtures by Khrushchev for rapprochement with Tito—was diminished greatly by the advent of the Warsaw Pact. Belgrade was suddenly confronted by an eight-member international treaty organization with implications for the diplomatic and economic isolation of Yugoslavia, and a convenient rationale for Soviet troop presence on Yugoslav borders. The avowed hostility of Warsaw Pact members toward Titoism became more threatening when the Pact began to improve its military preparedness after 1961.

Although the rupture of Soviet-Yugoslav relations has been recounted many times, we should recall that Tito's behavior from 1945 through 1947 was not, in rhetoric or in policy, anti-Soviet. Indeed, Stalin's inauguration of a new international—Cominform—in September 1947 had been suggested by Tito himself a couple years earlier. For Stalin, however, Tito's ideological conformity and rhetorical support of the USSR were insufficient. Stalin wanted, via Cominform, to stamp out any diversity in his newly acquired *cordon sanitaire*—a diversity personified by Tito. Brzezinski is certainly correct when he notes that Stalin was responsible for Titoism, by forcing the Yugoslav leader, who was convinced until the last that some accommodation for national autonomy could be found for a loyal party and ally, to find an ideological basis for differences.[37] Stalin's 1948 expulsion of Yugoslavia from the Cominform, because Tito refused to submit to a "far greater degree of Soviet involvement," launched Yugoslavia into a confrontation with the USSR that outlasted Tito and several Soviet leaders.[38]

Although Nikita Khrushchev tried—first in the 1955 Belgrade Declaration and again after the Twenty-first CPSU Congress in 1961—to reestablish cordial ties with Tito, the political effects of the Soviet-Warsaw Pact threat were clear. Yugoslavia had three sources of cohesion: Tito himself, the Yugoslav army, and the threat from the USSR and Moscow's East European allies. The "threat" has not necessarily been that of a Soviet invasion, but has always included "progressive internal disintegration being manipulated by skillful Soviet diplomacy, tactics and covert interference."[39] Of course, as we witnessed the socioeconomic and political deterioration of Yugoslavia in the 1980s, such internal disintegration became more and more plausible.

Notwithstanding the waxing and waning of Belgrade-Moscow ties over the past forty years, Tito and subsequent League of Communists of Yugoslavia (LCY) leaders have regarded their relationship with the USSR as one fraught with many risks. As a consequence, Yugoslavia has made an assiduous political and military effort to reinforce its security.

Politically and diplomatically Tito pressed for greater stability in the contiguous region while he carried his search for Yugoslav security worldwide. In the contiguous region, Tito and later LCY administrations sought to reduce potential conflicts with all neighbors. This regional political and diplomatic effort is not new. Yugoslav statesmen have always seen it to be in their best interest to encourage regional ties to counter the designs of outside interests. In the interwar period, the Yugoslavs were at the forefront of endeavors to create a "Balkan Union," in part because of their quite genuine fears of war with Fascist Italy. At the four Balkan Conferences in the early 1930s, and in the Balkan Pact signed by Yugoslavia, Turkey, Greece, and Romania on February 9, 1934, the Yugoslavs were particularly effusive about the possibilities for a Balkan Union.[40]

Two decades later, in the mid-1950s, in the aftermath of their expulsion from Cominform, the Yugoslavs again sought ways to limit the reach of powerful states—this time, of course, Soviet hegemony. Tito was cognizant of the limited nature of American (and, in general, Western) assistance, but also saw the need to initiate political cooperation with other anti-Soviet states in the Balkans. At Yugoslavia's initiative, the Turkish, Greek, and Yugoslav foreign ministers met in Ankara in early 1953, and the Ankara Treaty was signed in February.[41] This treaty laid the basis for a subsequent accord, another "Balkan Pact" signed in August 1954, which pledged each of the three signatories to "come to the defense of each other in the event of an outside attack."[42]

The Balkan Pact began to disintegrate soon after it was signed. Understandably, Greece and Turkey's preoccupation with NATO commitments (and increasingly concern about Cyprus and other bilateral disputes) were fundamentally incompatible with Tito's foreign and domestic policies. The USSR represented a threat to all three, but not the same kind of threat. Tito still hoped for party-to-party discussions, and for reconciliation with a post-Stalin Soviet leadership.

Apart from these ideologically induced doubts about where a Balkan Pact might lead, Tito also had begun in the mid-1950s to seek a broader framework in which to anchor Yugoslav security. It was Tito's "peripatetic summitry"[43] that launched what later became known as the Nonaligned Movement. With Gamal Abdul Nasser and Jawaharal Nehru, Tito brought twenty-five "Third-World" leaders to Belgrade in 1961 for the initial meeting of nonaligned states. This worldwide movement, until it was split with dissension in the 1970s, was of substantial benefit to Yugoslavia. Not only did the Nonaligned Movement enhance greatly Tito's and Yugoslavia's visibility, but the notion of nonalignment as distinct from neutrality brought substantial diplomatic attention and some degree of additional economic assistance. Tito, it is safe to presume, *did* see his worldwide endeavors on behalf of nonalignment as a contribution to his country's security vis-à-vis the USSR and the newly created Warsaw Pact.[44]

It can be argued, however, that the first Nonaligned Movement conference, held in Belgrade in 1961, represented the highpoint in Tito's effort to fashion a truly worldwide association of states opposed to military alliances. Particularly as many more newly independent, poor nation-states joined the movement, its focus began to shift from the issue that concerned Tito most—the dangers of military alliances led by superpowers—to the economic demands of the world's underdeveloped "South" versus the developed "North." In the 1970s, the involvement of a bloc of radical governments, led by Cuba, in the Nonaligned Movement pulled the organization further yet from issues that concerned Yugoslav security. It was evident at the Algiers meeting of the Nonaligned Movement in 1973 that what had begun, in part, as a Yugoslav counterweight to the superpower alliances around it (and to threats against Yugoslav security that could not be limited from within the Balkans) would not in the future serve that purpose.[45]

This diminishing relevance of nonalignment, per se, for Yugoslav security was also becoming clearer as Tito's death became increasingly expected and the implications of his passing for Yugoslav unity were brought into sharper focus. The Croatian crisis in 1971, indications of mounting ethnic tension in the south where Serbs confronted a population explosion of Albanians in Kosovo, and ominous signs that the economic boom of the 1960s was not going to continue, made Yugoslav domestic conditions seem far more vital than the distant issues of nonalignment. East-West "detente" of the early to mid-1970s also appeared to reduce the security need for a worldwide Yugoslav commitment. In his final years, Tito continued to seek a Nonaligned Movement true to its original purposes, and under his guidance Yugoslavia remained firmly committed to such a movement.[46] For the LCY and the army, however, it had become clear that the real challenges for Yugoslavia's future were within and nearby. In December 1979, moreover, it was demonstrated brutally in Afghanistan that nonalignment, in any case, was no guarantee against Soviet intervention and occupation.

There was, as well, the irredentist issue of Macedonia raised by Bulgaria, which had been omnipresent throughout the postwar period. Although this has been a less active issue than, for example, the Romanian-Hungarian diatribe concerning Transylvania, or Greek-Turkish confrontations, the Yugoslavs have seen the Bulgarian claims in terms of possible scenarios for a larger conflict with the Soviets.[47] The Macedonian issue has recurred recently in the Greek-Bulgarian accord of September 1986 and in 1990 as Sofia and Athens again moved closer with high-level diplomatic visits. From Belgrade's perspective, clauses in the protocol that promise Greek-Bulgarian cooperation against externally sponsored "agitation or action that might imperil" Greek or Bulgarian stability are clearly directed against not just Turkish-Moslem minorities in both countries, but also against the Macedonian nationalism that is politically visible in Skopje.[48]

Yugoslav participation in the 1976 all-Balkan (except Albania) conference in Athens was a move toward refocusing Yugoslav diplomatic efforts on Southeastern Europe and the Eastern Mediterranean, perhaps to use regional cooperation as a deterrent against Soviet designs whenever Tito died.[49] The Yugoslav role in the Conference for Security and Cooperation in Europe (CSCE) reflected a desire to maintain the Helsinki momentum for similar reasons—to strengthen relations with Western Europe and to reinforce European recognition of Yugoslavia's importance. Belgrade hosted the 1977–1978 CSCE Review Conference and was active as well at the CSCE Review Conference in Madrid (1980–1981) and the meeting in Stockholm in 1985–1986, which resulted in significant expansion of confidence and security-building measures first included in the Helsinki Accord.[50] Throughout 1986 and 1987 the Yugoslav foreign ministry devoted considerable effort to bring together all Balkan foreign ministers (including Albania's) in a session that reflected former Prime Minister Branko Mikulic's conviction that these efforts at regional political rapprochement and diplomatic contacts have priority.[51]

These new priorities for Yugoslav foreign policy and the notion that the country's security may best be obtained through links with Western

Europe and diplomatic initiatives in the Balkans, were not the products of farsightedness among LCY politicians. Rather, "party officials, intellectuals and the press" had increasingly criticized Belgrade after Tito's death "for its persistent policy of supporting third-world interests at the expense of strengthening economic relations with the highly developed nations of Western Europe [and for] not improving relations with the country's Balkan neighbors."[52] Moreover, as the Yugoslav army observed mounting ethnic unrest and worker discontent, one can well imagine a defense minister (as did Branko Mamula) warning civilian LCY politicians of the immediate internal dangers to state security and the army's impatience with the party's capacity to address problems at home.[53]

The Soviet threat to Yugoslavia, and the possible implementation of intervention through the multilateral facade of the Warsaw Pact, is far less today because of Mikhail Gorbachev. Gorbachev's visit to Yugoslavia in March 1988 was, like his visits elsewhere, impressive. From the standpoint of Yugoslavia security, he took care to say all the right things—especially by repeating his views about the inviolable right of people to "shape their own destiny."[54]

The changes in the USSR, Soviet military withdrawals from Eastern Europe, and an improved climate of superpower relations—coming at a time when Yugoslavia is confronted by clear and present dangers to its survival from antagonism between Serbs and Slovenes or Croatians, violent clashes between Albanians and Serbs, rampant corruption and a leadership vacuum—have created an environment for Yugoslavs to worry far less about external threats. This has not meant any talk about altering military doctrine or security planning, although reductions of Yugoslav army force levels have been discussed and probably will be effected. Nevertheless, the international political context at the beginning of the 1990s suggests little that is ominous, because for most residents of Yugoslavia everything that appears ominous lies within their own country.

Albania

Albania, which joined the Warsaw Pact when it was founded in 1955, officially withdrew in 1968. During this brief association with the Pact, the alliance provided little utility for Enver Hoxha, and the multilateral facade of the Pact added nothing to Soviet influence over Albania. The WTO's effects on Albania were, however, felt in less direct ways.

Albania was the only country in Eastern Europe where the Communist Party came to power without assistance from the Soviet army. Yet the Communist regime in Albania could not have succeeded without substantial assistance from the Yugoslav Communists, who sent advisers to the Albanian Communist Party during the war, and troops and economic assistance to the Albanians when the war ended. Tito planned, it appeared, to include Albania in a Balkan union under his control.[55] When Stalin expelled Yugoslavia from the Cominform in 1948, it was an opportunity for Hoxha to escape from one patron into the arms of another.

Implicit in this new dependence on Moscow was a heightened Soviet profile in Albania. From Moscow's standpoint, Albania provided diplomatic and military leverage against Tito, and served as an important base from which to operate in the Eastern Mediterranean. Soviet submarines began to use the port at Valona,[56] and large Soviet-sponsored industrial projects were launched in Albania. After Albania joined in the Warsaw Pact, the treaty provided an ex post facto, multilateral justification for Soviet presence in Albania, which, of course, was directed against Tito as much as against NATO.

The Soviet-Albanian dispute, which broke out several years later, had at its core Hoxha's dislike of Khrushchev's "revisionism" and the Soviet's extreme displeasure at close Albanian-Chinese relations.[57] By October 1961, Khrushchev was calling for the removal of the Albanian leadership. Hoxha responded by throwing out Soviet advisers and closing the submarine base at Valona.[58]

The Albanians nevertheless delayed their departure from the Warsaw Pact until after the Soviet invasion of Czechoslovakia in 1968. Several reasons for this delay seem plausible: (1) The Albanians may have believed that continued nominal membership in the Warsaw Pact was needed as a balance against the Yugoslavs. (2) The Albanian leadership may have anticipated the demise of Khrushchev, and hoped for a return to Soviet neo-Stalinism. And (3), as James Brown speculates, Tirana may have felt safer vis-à-vis the Soviets inside rather than outside the Warsaw Pact, *until* the Soviet-led Warsaw Pact action to end the "Prague Spring" in August 1968.[59]

From 1968 until the death of Mao Zedong in 1976, the Albanian leadership used the implicit threat of Soviet/Warsaw Pact intervention to extract very large amounts of economic and military assistance from the Chinese.[60] Chinese largesse was based on Tirana's ideological support for Maoism, and the not inconsiderable Albanian reserves of a strategic metal such as chromium. At the same time, Albania provided an entree to the USSR's "backyard" for the Chinese—a component of a larger strategic game between the two principal Communist Party states. For Albania, the alliance with China served as a deterrent against an extension of the Brezhnev Doctrine beyond states contiguous to the USSR, as well as a means to gain economic and military assistance without significant cost.

Mao's death in 1976, and the reemergence of Deng Xiaoping by 1978 to become the principal figure in Chinese politics, led to a cooling of relations. In July 1978 China cut off aid to Albania, the culmination of growing disagreements between the two countries over foreign policy and questions of revolutionary principles.

During the next seven years, Albania evinced antipathy toward everyone. Hoxha's regime scorned all major powers and most of Albania's neighbors (although there were tentative conciliatory steps with Greece and Italy). The safety of Albania was assured through its relative isolation and its insignificance to the great powers.

Hoxha's own death in April 1985, however, raised questions about the directions of Albanian domestic and foreign policy. Such a small and poor country, undergoing a rapid expansion of its population,[61] needs developmental assistance and markets for the products it can export. The direction taken by Ramiz Alia has been to resurrect ties with Western states, including those that are NATO members,[62] and the return of Albania to international forums. Prime Minister Carcani and Foreign Minister Malile have actively tried to remove obstacles to the normalization of relations with the rest of Europe. For example, after more than a year of discussion concerning territorial disputes and the large Greek minority in Albania, the official state of war between Greece and Albania (dating from World War II) was finally ended in 1987.[63] In October 1987, formal diplomatic relations with West Germany were instituted, and a September 1988 visit by Foreign Minister Malile to Bonn broke new ground with a wide-ranging cultural agreement between Albania and West Germany.

Substantial economic and cultural cooperation has also begun with Turkey, and contacts with other West European states have been initiated.[64] With ties to Turkey becoming warmer, principal frictions with Athens removed, and an evident willingness to participate in regional discussions such as the Balkan foreign ministers' conference early in 1988, it seems clear that Albanian policy is directed toward ensuring its own security rather than relying solely on finding a new patron. Significantly, Tirana hosted its first multilateral diplomatic conference since World War II in January 1989, when deputy foreign ministers from the six Balkan states convened for a follow-up session to the 1988 Belgrade meeting.

If the Albanian Communist regime has external security concerns today, they will not be focused on Warsaw Pact members or the USSR itself. Albanian diplomacy began to probe in 1986 the possibilities of bilateral accords with NSWP communist states then still resisting reform. The first crack in decades of Albanian–Warsaw Pact hostility came in the summer of 1986, when a major trade accord was signed between Albania and East Germany, and a ministerial-level East German delegation came to Tirana for a meeting with Prime Minister Adil Carcani.[65] Albania's unremitting hostility toward Warsaw Pact states then waned.

Tirana did not, however, respond quickly to the nudges from Moscow to normalize relations.[66] The strategic retreat of the USSR in 1989–1990 has, of course, added to the Albanian regime's perception that no threat lies to the East, and relations with Moscow were finally renewed in the summer of 1990. Security concerns, however, now must focus on immediate neighbors.

Yugoslavia, particularly now that Serbian nationalism has become personified by the Serbian party leader Slobodan Milosevic, represents a continued threat, and there is ample vitriol in Alia's rhetoric about Yugoslav treatment of Albanian nationals in Kosovo or elsewhere. Yet it is unlikely that Albanian leaders envisage a military confrontation with Yugoslavia. Recent events in Kosovo have nevertheless led to a serious deterioration in Yugoslav-Albanian relations.

For Albanian foreign policy, the Warsaw Pact played a number of peripheral but nevertheless significant roles. The Pact was a signal of Soviet protection against Yugoslavia and potential cover for Soviet intervention. At all times, the WTO has been a thin veneer for Soviet strategic interests that affected Albania deeply. In the past decade, as Soviet attention was drawn away from the Balkans, Albania has avoided a new patron. Since Hoxha's death, Albania has used an independent foreign policy as a means for security rather than seeking a return to the dependence that has characterized Albanian existence for decades.

The Soviet Union and Southeastern Europe

Notwithstanding extraordinary effort over many years, the Soviets failed to achieve their goals in Southeastern Europe. In Romania, Ceausescu used the Soviet/Warsaw Pact presence for many years to rally public support for his autocratic regime. The USSR implored Warsaw Pact states to increase defense spending, maintain manpower levels, and undertake more performance effort (maneuvers, etc.), with only limited success. Bulgaria still confronts issues of loyalty in the army and ethnic tension in the population. Yugoslavia under Tito was not intimidated by the Soviets and Warsaw Pact, and gained international stature by anchoring Yugoslav security in the Nonaligned Movement. Albania, emerging from self-imposed isolation, has spurned reintegration with the USSR and focused on improving relations with Western Europe and democratic states in Southeastern Europe.

Why did the Soviets failed to achieve better results? What accounts for the inability of the USSR to have used effectively instruments at its disposal—most notably the Warsaw Pact—to mold the Communist states of Southeastern Europe into a compliant and impermeable "Southern Tier" of a Soviet *cordon sanitaire* during the 1970s and 1980s?

In Southeastern Europe the Soviet efforts to create a closely knit alliance encountered a number of obstacles. In Yugoslavia and Albania, genuine leaders emerged from the war whose own legitimacy was only enhanced by Soviet attempts at intimidation. In the Yugoslav and Albanian cases, transit through other states was necessary before Soviet forces could be used against them. Romania, Yugoslavia, and Albania also adopted territorial defense strategies that eschewed prolonged conventional combat by their countries' standing armies if the Soviets or Warsaw Pact neighbors attacked. Such military doctrines added greatly to the uncertain consequences of intervention, and raised the possibility that very large occupation forces would be tied down by indigenous partisan armies.

The USSR's inability to maintain tight control over most of the Communist states of Southeastern Europe also had much to do with the kinds of centrifugal tendencies present in the region. From 1956 until the latter 1980s, none of the political changes in the Balkans challenged the leading role of the party. Events of such magnitude finally *did* occur in the region, but other constraints on Soviet/Warsaw Pact intervention had come first, and there was little Moscow could do.

It is often argued that Southeastern Europe lacks the strategic importance for the Soviet Union of Central and Northern Europe. The argument is used to explain Moscow's decisions to allow Albania to walk away from the Warsaw Pact, to let Romania's deviance run its course, and to accept Hungary's failure to live up to the performance requirements of "core" Warsaw Pact members all long before the destruction of communist rule.[67] At the same time, the Southern Tier may have become less critical to the Soviets *because* of Tito, Albania's defection, and Romanian intransigence. Certainly, Russian historical interest in the Bosporus and Dardanelles is well understood, and the desire to protect Russian interests in the Balkans is well-established in historical experience.

Crediting nationalism for Moscow's inability to ensure its unquestioned dominance in Communist Southeastern Europe may likewise lead us astray. Certainly, the nationalism of Romanians was never any stronger than that of the Hungarians in 1956 or Czechs in 1968. The nature of Romania's differences from Warsaw Pact norms and the creation of a territorial defense strategy, however, were probably stronger deterrents to Soviet action than any measure of popular devotion to the nation.

Military Doctrine

Among the four states in Southeastern Europe that were ruled by communist parties until 1989, plus Hungary, there have been five distinct orientations for national military policy in the past two decades (roughly since the invasion of Czechoslovakia and the reorganization of the Pact in early 1969). Although Romania and Bulgaria have been Warsaw Pact members throughout that period, their military policies have followed different directions. For want of better terms, I categorize these different policies, with Hungary as a third and intriguing comparison, as follows:

1. "Nominal Warsaw Pact"—Romania, which adopted a territorial defense strategy while refusing to participate in joint maneuvers, denying transit to Soviet troops, and withdrawing from officer education programs in the USSR;
2. "Peripheral Warsaw Pact"—Hungary, which adopted no doctrine that deviates from Warsaw Pact norms prior to 1989–1990, but lowered its military commitments to levels below any other integrated Pact member. (In 1990, of course, the Hungarian Parliament passed a bill to withdraw the country from WTO);
3. "Total Warsaw Pact"—Bulgaria, the military doctrine and defense economy of which were entirely absorbed into the coalitional warfare rubric of the Warsaw Pact for several decades.

In addition, of course, the two non-Warsaw Pact Communist states adopted military doctrines that distinguished them in other ways:

4. "Non-Warsaw Pact Autonomous Territorial Defense"—Yugoslavia (and Albania post 1978), where a largely independent effort, based on historical experience, is made to prepare standing army, paramilitary, and irregular troops to engage in a war of the entire people against an invader;
5. "Non-Warsaw Pact Externally Dependent Territorial Defense"—Albania, early 1960s through 1978, in which a major power provides the bulk of weapons and the ultimate guarantee of a territorial defense strategy's validity.

Although all five military doctrines reflect different adaptations to opportunities, options, or the lack thereof, *all* were heavily influenced by the existence of the Warsaw Pact and its transparent roles within Eastern Europe. Were there no Warsaw Pact, Soviet bilateral ties alone could have provided justification for neither Bulgaria's burdensome military effort nor Soviet absorption of Bulgaria's defense economy. Now, with a Pact that is but a shadow of its former self, this difficulty has begun to plague Bulgarian decision-makers. In Hungary, where the population long ago had decided that the Warsaw Pact was "expendable and a hindrance,"[68] even a modest military effort by East European standards would be difficult to extract were the Soviets present without any multilateral element. Hungary's rapid reduction of force levels to perhaps no more than 70,000 speaks of this desire to demilitarize. For Romania, Yugoslavia, and Albania, of course, the potential for Soviet or NSWP invasions was behind the original development of territorial defense strategies—although Albania's preparations were directed as well against Yugoslavia.

These five paths for military policies among states in the region, while they were all ruled by communist parties, thus reflect varying points along a continuum largely defined by the degree of domestic turmoil and the extent of tension between the USSR and each Balkan state.

Regional Security Issues

As discussed in country-specific observations of the preceding section, few of the burning security issues of the Balkans were caused by, or could have been solved by, the Warsaw Pact. Yet the Soviet security involvement, if only through a state's nominal Warsaw Pact membership, affects the disposition of these regional issues. Leaving aside Greek-Turkish conflicts, several significant issues may engender confrontations between states of the region. All involve post-communist states, and most involve at least one Warsaw Pact member. These areas of real and potential conflict include the following:

- Hungary versus Romania regarding the Hungarian minority in Transylvania and Transylvania in general as a territorial issue, with debates raging about historical settlement of Transylvania and emotions high concerning Hungarian charges of Romanian human-rights violations;
- Albania versus Yugoslavia concerning Albanians in Kosovo and Serbian treatment of them there and in other republics, with Yugoslavia viewing Albanian statements as provocative interference;
- Bulgaria versus Romania regarding Dobrudja, a territory on the Black Sea coast divided between Romania and Bulgaria which Bulgaria claims entirely for itself while asserting that ethnic Bulgarians who reside in the Romanian part have been denied socioeconomic and political opportunities;
- Albania versus Greece, with the issue being the Greek minority inside Albanian territory ("Northern Epirus," according to the Greeks);[69]
- Romania versus the USSR concerning Moldavia SSR, where the Romanian language is spoken by ⅔ of the population and which Romanians see as rightfully theirs;
- Greece versus Yugoslavia regarding Macedonia, which Greeks assert does not exist, and never existed;

Security in the Balkans

- Bulgaria versus Yugoslavia (particularly Serbia), alleging Belgrade's sponsorship of resurgent Macedonian nationalist groups inside Bulgaria.

In the most notable recent example, Hungarians reacted bitterly not only to the continued political repression of the Hungarian minority in Romania during the 1980s, but also to the ex-dictator Ceausescu's plan to destroy thousands of villages (many of them Hungarian in order to modernize Romanian agriculture.)[70] Hungarian interests, had the Warsaw Pact not been present, would have required that demands be made for the protection of its minorities and punitive action if those demands were not met. In the Warsaw Pact environment, however, there were constraints on military or economic retaliation, and substantial disincentives to bringing the dispute to the UN. Now that Ceausescu is gone, the WTO dormant, and Hungary democratic, more not less potential exists for volatility if Budapest and Bucharest politicians think there is something to gain from nationalist outbursts.

Communist countries of Southeastern Europe pursued matters of national interest and security, always being affected by the Warsaw Pact's existence, reminding participants in disputes of Soviet interests. In the case of Hungary, for example, we can well appreciate the pithy observation by Peter Bender that "Hungary's security problem, so far as it is of a military kind, consists solely in its membership [in] the Warsaw Pact."[71] Hungary's effort in 1990–1991, of course, is to eliminate that security problem. But in doing so, other issues may be allowed to become much more acute.

Conclusion

As ideologically based blocs decayed in Europe, old bilateral, nationally rooted issues regained importance in Southeastern Europe. Little of the evidence presented here would suggest a large role for the USSR in Southeastern Europe in settling these disputes. There are few scenarios in which Moscow, with Gorbachev or any foreseeable leadership, would be inclined to intervene militarily in the region—and only in the most extreme case of an anti-Russian irredentism in neighboring Romania or Bulgaria would the probability of armed intervention rise significantly during the 1990s.

The principal security orientation of Southeastern Europe—that is, where and how the states of the region seek to enhance their military, political, and economic capacities vis-à-vis adversaries—will be through ties with the European Community and the CSCE process, augumented by bilateral and regional arrangements. For almost four decades after

World War II, the USSR loomed as the principal threat or overwhelming ally of Balkan states. In the 1980s, and more so in the 1990s, a resurgence of intraregional and national quarrels, the perceptible withdrawal of the USSR to tend to grievous domestic problems, and the advent in 1992 of European economic unity together imply strong currents pushing the security orientation of Southeastern Europe away from what we have known for decades. The relationship between the USSR and Balkan post-communist states will increasingly be defined by these countries' own interests. The Pact itself is unlikely to disband entirely, but will be of minimal utility to the USSR as a means of guaranteeing its security. At conventional arms control talks in Vienna, of course, the Warsaw Pact will remain on the diplomatic stage, but the Pact will be a fiction relative to tangible priorities of each state which would have been unthinkable in the past.

Bulgaria's fealty to Moscow is unlikely to change dramatically, but a genuine *Bulgarian* perspective on its own security focusing on a Turkish threat, rapprochement with Greece, and increased involvement in Balkan and European diplomacy, has now emerged. For Romania, the USSR appears to pose a military threat only insofar as a crisis over Moldovia could take on dramatic proportions (e.g., through border incidents). The new Iliescu-Roman government may well see its greatest external security danger emerging from Hungary and the indictments of Romanian minority policies. A post-Ceausescu Romania will not simply reintegrate itself within Soviet security planning, but will instead try to find ways to repair socioeconomic losses of the Ceausescu era via reconciliation with the European Community while placating Soviet concerns. For Yugoslavia, with its own dissolution at issue, external "threats" pale by comparison. Only the West can help economically; added Soviet involvement would solve nothing. For Albania, only Yugoslavia poses any "threat," and the Warsaw Pact or the USSR are largely irrelevant to the Kosovo dilemma. Certainly, the USSR has proved to be no model for resolving ethnic/national disputes.

In the years ahead, as the trauma of Yugoslavia unfolds, both Romania and Bulgaria cope with tenuous governments, and Albania continues to emerge from decades of isolation, there will be little room for a Soviet reassertion of a multilateral or superpower security perspective in the Balkans. Obviously, the USSR will make every effort to have its interests and preferences known, using diplomatic visibility, military aid and credits, and energy and raw material exports as leverage. Aside from weapons and raw materials, however, Moscow's tools with which to impose its "will"—assuming, of course, that the Soviets had the wherewithal to make such an effort—are incomplete.

Southeastern Europe needs capital investment to modernize, not just raw material imports to fuel existing industry. Southeastern Europe has little need for advanced weaponry that the USSR might export, and Yugoslavia and Romania have well-developed small-arms industries of their own. And Southeastern Europe is likely to view the USSR's capacity for sustained military intervention as less credible in the 1990s than in the 1960s or 1970s.

The historical cleavages of Southeastern Europe have, instead, penetrated and "overcome" the veneer of late-twentieth-century alliances. Superpower-led or imposed treaty organizations affected, but did not determine, the course of post–World War II political-military affairs in the region bounded by the Black Sea, Aegean, and Adriatic. That diverse forms of one-party authoritarianism and an array of defense and international policies all developed within the geographic confines of four states in Southeastern Europe suggests the limits of power for superpowers and their military alliances. Those limits will only become more pronounced in the post-communist era.

Notes

1. Helene Carrere d'Encausse, in her book *Big Brother: The Soviet Union and Eastern Europe* (London: Holmes and Meier, 1987), p. 269, states that "the Pact had as its primary function to demonstrate that the socialist camp existed and that it could not be changed."

2. Viktor Kulikov, ed., *Varshavskii Dogovor: Soiuz vo imia mira i sotsializma* (Moscow: Voenizdat, 1980), contains discussion of these early stages of the Pact and, implicitly, its inactivity.

3. Particularly in the spring and summer of 1971, numerous Soviet and Soviet-Bulgarian-Hungarian exercises were clearly meant to signal to Ceausescu the limits to his behavior. Ceausescu's close contacts with China may have been the "final straw" that led Brezhnev to such demonstrative warnings. In any case, it is certain that Ceausescu was worried and anticipated the worst. See, for instance, the speeches in mid-August 1971 contained in the collection of Ceausescu's pronouncements, *Romania on the Way of Building Up the Multilaterally Developed Socialist Society* (Bucharest: Meridian Publishing House, 1972), pp. 271–302.

4. For example, Jeffrey Simon counts "no less than seven exercises around [Romania's] borders" in the two years from the summer of 1969 through the early fall of 1971. See his account of these maneuvers and the threatening posture toward Romania (and Yugoslavia) in Jeffrey Simon, *Warsaw Pact Forces* (Boulder, Colo.: Westview Press, 1985), pp. 83–87.

5. One must, of course, give credit to Ceausescu's political acumen, as Michael Shafir does, when accounting for his success in moving aside holdovers from the Gheorghiu-Dej years. See Michael Shafir, *Romania* (London: Frances Pinter, 1985). Yet the Standing Presidium (i.e., Politburo) and the larger Political Executive

30   *Security in the Balkans*

Committee had remained unchanged from the Ninth Congress (July 1965) through the end of 1967, and 1969 saw departures of the Gheorghiu-Dej cohort from these bodies, with further changes at the Tenth Congress in August 1969. Certainly, the coincidence of Ceausescu's popularity and tie to nationalism in the face of Soviet/Warsaw Pact threat helped to make his position unassailable.

6. The "initial decisions [to fight alongside the Germans in their 1941 invasion of the USSR] were not unpopular," writes Barbara Jelavich. The "general public acceptance," however, was focused on the need to regain Bukovina and Bessarabia, which the Soviets had annexed a year earlier, and on the need to gain German approval for a return of that part of Transylvania ceded to Hungary via German "arbitration" in 1940. Furthermore, Romanians' "animosity was directed against their Soviet neighbor and had its base in . . . historical conflict" Jelavich, *History of the Balkans: Twentieth Century* (Cambridge: Cambridge University Press, 1983), pp. 250–251.

7. See, for example, Mary Ellen Fischer, "Idol or Leader? The Origins and Future of the Ceausescu Cult," in Daniel N. Nelson, ed., *Romania in the 1980s* (Boulder, Colo.: Westview Press, 1981).

8. "Cuvintare la intilnire cu representanti ai clasei muncitoare," November 25, 1978; "Cuvintare la intilnire cu representanti ai taranimii, intelectualitatii, si tineretului," November 25, 1978; "Cuvintare la intilnire cu representanti ai armata si ai ministeriul de interna," November 27, 1978 (Bucharest: Editura Politica, 1978). The first two of these speeches were also carried in *Scinteia* (November 26, 1978), 1 and 3.

9. I have discussed specific aspects of the deteriorating socioeconomic conditions of the late Ceausescu period in Daniel N. Nelson, "The Romanian Disaster," in T. Anthony Jones, ed., *Research on the Soviet Union and Eastern Europe* (Cambridge, Mass: JAI Press, 1990).

10. These data are gathered by professional polling organizations on behalf of Radio Free Europe through continuous sampling, over three-year periods, of East European nationals traveling to Western Europe. Findings are reported in Radio Free Europe, East European Audience and Opinion Research, "Political Legitimacy in Eastern Europe: A Comparative Study" (March 1987), Table 6, p. 18. For Romania, specifically, negative evaluations of the performance of the Ceausescu regime increased drastically as a proportion of all responses in the late 1970s. Indeed what I have termed a "negative shift" of public opinion was larger in Romania than anywhere in the Warsaw Pact. See Daniel N. Nelson, "Osteuropaischer Kommunismus und offentliche Meinung," in *Europa Archiv* (December, 1988).

11. R.F.E. Background Report, "Rumanian Difficulties in Military and Security Affairs" (March 6, 1972).

12. Aurel Braun, *Romanian Foreign Policy Since 1965* (New York: Praeger, 1978), pp. 154–155.

13. B.B.C. Summary of World Broadcasts (December 16, 1982).

14. I have discussed these data and their implications in "Military Policies and Military Politics" in Daniel N. Nelson, *Romanian Politics in the Ceausescu Era* (New York: Gordon and Breach, 1989).

Security in the Balkans 31

15. As public approval began to plummet in the early to mid-1980s (see sources cited in note 10), Romanian military expenditures as a proportion of GNP, central government expenditures, and per capita spending, as well as force levels as a proportion of population, all rose. The most dramatic increases were in 1982 and 1983, with 1984 and 1985 data indicating that the military effort was maintained even as the economic crisis lessened slightly. For data on military expenditures consult U.S. Arms Control and Disarmament Agency (ACDA), *World Military Expenditures and Arms Transfers* (Washington, D.C.: ACDA, 1987) [Hereafter "ACDA"], p. 74.

16. Henry Kamm, "For Bucharest, a Great Leap Backward," *New York Times* (February 15, 1988).

17. Nicolae Ceausescu, as quoted in *Scinteia* (May 4, 1988).

18. See, for example, William Echikson, "Hungarian Refugees Spark Rare East-bloc Row," *Christian Science Monitor* (June 13, 1988); and Echikson, "Hungarians Protest Romanian Plan to Destroy Villages," *Christian Science Monitor* (June 27, 1988).

19. See my discussion of the officer corps' likely attitudes in "Military Politics and Military Policies in Ceausescu's Romania" in Daniel N. Nelson, *Romanian Politics in the Ceausescu Era,* op. cit.

20. Rankings of Bulgarian expenditures and manpower levels relative to all nation-states reveal this surprisingly high and consistent commitment. See, for example, ACDA, p. 51, for raw data, and p. 38 for Bulgaria's rankings in 1985. For instance, Bulgaria ranked twelfth in the world in military expenditures per capita and sixteenth in armed forces as a proportion of population, that is, above the 90th percentile of all nation-states on both indicators. One should note, moreover, that those rankings are *after* a modest decline in Bulgarian military effort generally from the late 1970s into the 1980s.

21. Regarding Bulgaria's economic performance, see George R. Feiwel, "Industrialization" in Stephen Fisher-Galati, ed., *Eastern Europe in the 1980s* (Boulder, Colo.: Westview Press, 1982), pp. 55–82; NMP data are from Thad P. Alton, "East European GNPs: Origins of Product, Final Uses, Rates of Growth and International Comparisons." In Joint Economic Committee, *East European Economies: Slow Growth in the 1980s* (Washington, D.C.: U.S. Government Printing Office, 1985), pp. 115–116.

22. Central Intelligence Agency, Directorate of Intelligence, *Handbook of Economic Statistics* (Washington, D.C.: C.I.A., 1986) [Hereafter, "CIA"], pp. 101–102 and p. 130.

23. *Narodna Armiya* (December 12, 1984), as translated in FBIS *Daily Report, Eastern Europe* (December 17, 1984).

24. ACDA, 1984, 1985, 1986, 1987.

25. CIA, 1987, pp. 212, 222.

26. John D. Bell, *The Bulgarian Communist Party from Blagoev to Zhivkov* (Stanford: Hoover Institution Press, 1986); see also, John Jaworsky, "Bulgaria" in Teresa Rakowska-Harmstone et al., *Warsaw Pact; The Question of Cohesion,* Phase II, vol. 3 (Ottawa: Ministry of Defense, ORAE, 1985).

27. G.F. Vorontsov, *Voennye Koalitsii i Koalitsionnye Voiny* (Moscow: Voenizdat, 1976).

32 *Security in the Balkans*

28. Bell, p. 86; see also Nissan Oren, *Revolution Administered* (Baltimore: Johns Hopkins University Press, 1972), p. 86.

29. James F. Brown, *Bulgaria Under Communist Rule* (New York: Praeger, 1970), p. 179.

30. Michael Costello, "Bulgaria," in Adam Bromke and Teresa Rakowska-Harmstone, eds., *The Communist States in Disarray* (Minneapolis: University of Minnesota Press, 1972), p. 149; see also Brown, *Bulgaria Under Communist Rule,* pp. 173–187, for the most complete account of the conspiracy and its aftermath.

31. General Velichko Georgiev as quoted in *Narodna Armiya* (June 12, 1960).

32. See, for example, an editorial in *Narodna Armiya* (December 12, 1984).

33. Radio Free Europe, *Situation Reports—Bulgaria* no. 14 (October 23, 1984), pp. 1–4; see also Radio Free Europe, *Background Report* no. 150 (December 27, 1985), p. 12.

34. See reports on the ethnic unrest and Turkish claims in the *New York Times* (May 19, 1985 and August 5, 1985).

35. Stephen Ashley, "Bulgaria and the Balkan Foreign Ministers' Conference," Radio Free Europe Research, Vol 13, no. 10 (March 11, 1988), *Bulgarian Situation Report,* no. 3 (March 8, 1988), p. 6.

36. Ashley, "Bulgaria and the Balkan Foreign Ministers' Conference," pp. 5–8.

37. Zbigniew Brzezinski, *The Soviet Bloc* (Cambridge, Mass.: Harvard University Press, 1967), pp. 62–64.

38. Ibid., p. 64.

39. James F. Brown, *Eastern Europe and Communist Rule* (Durham, N.C.: Duke University Press, 1988), p.363.

40. T.I. Geshkoff, *Balkan Union* (New York: Columbia University Press, 1940); see also a brief discussion of the Balkan conferences and ancillary cooperation during the 1930s in Ioan Mircea Pascu, "The Balkans: A Romanian Perspective," in David Carlton and Carlo Schaerf, eds., *South-Eastern Europe After Tito* (New York: St. Martin's Press, 1983), pp. 137–140.

41. Aurel Brown, *Small State Security in the Balkans* (Totawa, N.J.: Barnes and Noble, 1983), p. 44.

42. Hans Gunter Brauch, "Confidence-Building Measures in the Balkans and the Eastern Mediterranean," in Carlton and Schaerf, eds., *South-Eastern Europe After Tito,* p. 46.

43. Ronald Linden, *Communist States and International Change* (New York: Allen and Unwin, 1986), p.12.

44. Braun, *Small State Security in the Balkans,* p. 46.

45. Changes within the Nonaligned Movement toward North-South issues and the attempt by radical states to view the USSR and Warsaw Pact states as the "natural partner" of nonalignment are discussed by Richard L. Jackson, *The Non-Aligned, the U.N., and the Superpowers* (New York: Praeger, 1983), pp. 24–36. Generally, as well, see Ernest Corea, *Non-Alignment: Dynamics of A Movement* (Toronto: Canadian Institute of International Affairs, 1977).

46. Works devoted specifically to Tito and Yugoslavia's role are Alvin Z. Rubinstein, *Yugoslavia and the Nonaligned World* (Princeton, N.J.: Princeton

Security in the Balkans 33

University Press, 1970); and *Tito and the Non-Aligned Movement* (Belgrade: Socialist Thought and Practice), especially pp. 75–92 with Tito's speech to the Algiers conference in 1973.

47. Paul Shoup, *Communism and the Yugoslav National Question* (New York: Columbia University Press, 1968), pp. 144–183.

48. Stephen Asley, "Greek-Bulgaria Friendship Treaty," in Vojtech Mastny, ed., *Soviet-East European Survey, 1986–1987* (Boulder, Colo.: Westview Press, 1987), pp. 318–325.

49. Braun, *Small-State Security in the Balkans,* p. 52.

50. Regarding Yugoslav involvement in the CSCE process, and the specific issue of confidence-building measures, see Hans Gunter Brauch, *Vertrauensbildende* (Gerlingen: Bliecher, 1986).

51. The Balkan foreign ministers' conference of February 24–26, 1988 was arranged and hosted by the Yugoslavs. Yugoslav Foreign Minister (now Vice President in the State Presidency) Raif Dizdarevic issued formal invitations of April 6, 1987, in a letter to his four counterparts. Tanjung dispatch, April 22, 1987.

52. Milan Andrejevich, "The Balkan Foreign Ministers' Conference from the Yugoslav Angle," Radio Free Europe Research, *Yugoslav Situation Report,* no. 2 (March 10, 1988), p. 6.

53. Defense Minister Branko Mamula, interview in *Narodna Armija* (September 23, 1987).

54. In a speech to Yugoslav Federal Assembly, in Belgrade on March 16, 1988, Gorbachev noted that "democratization requires an unconditional recognition by the international community of the right of each people to shape its destiny, its right to dispose of its own resources. This is a universal, general right. It cannot belong to some 'chosen' peoples, and the more so be measured by the economic or military potential of states . . . each people has its interests that are not subordinated to the interests of other states." See Tass dispatch, March 16, 1988, as cited in *News and Views From the USSR,* distributed by the Soviet Embassy, Washington, D.C. This statement, in direct contrast to the so-called Brezhnev Doctrine, was well received.

55. Jelavich, *History of the Balkans,* p. 274.

56. Michael McCGwire, *Soviet Naval Developments* (New York: Praeger, 1975), p. 345.

57. One standard source that describes events from the late 1950s through the early 1960s is William E. Griffith, *Albania and the Sino-Soviet Rift* (Cambridge, Mass.: MIT Press, 1963). Other useful sources, with details about the long Chinese-Albanian relationship, are Peter R. Prifti, *Socialist Albania Since 1944: Domestic and Foreign Developments* (Cambridge, Mass.: MIT Press, 1978), and Berhard Tonnes, *Sonderfall Albanien* (Munchen: F. Oldenburg, 1980).

58. Braun, *Small-State Security in the Balkans,* p. 38.

59. Brown, *Eastern Europe and Communist Rule,* p. 373.

60. Michael Kaser, "Trade and Aid in the Albanian Economy," in U.S. Congress, Joint Economic Committee, *East European Economics Post-Helsinki* (Washington, D.C.: U.S. Government Printing Office, 1977).

61. For a general analysis of Albania's socioeconomic and political conditions, including issues of food production and population growth, consult Michael Kaser, *Albania Under and After Enver Hoxha* (Washington, D.C.: U.S. Congress, Joint Economic Committee, 1986).

62. For a discussion of these foreign-policy options shortly after Hoxha's death, see Elez Biberaj, "Albania After Hoxha: Dilemmas of Change," *Problems of Communism,* vol. XXXIV (November–December 1985), especially pp. 41–46.

63. Brown, *Eastern Europe and Communist Rule,* p. 380.

64. For example, discussions between Albania and Britain, in part over the Corfu incident more than four decades ago, were resumed in secret after Hoxha's death—although noted in the press. See J. Cooley, "Albania Expected to Resume Secret Talks with Britain," *Christian Science Monitor* (August 26, 1985).

65. Louis Zanga, "Reform Albanian Style," in Vojtech Mastny, ed., *Soviet-East European Survey, 1986-1987,* p. 297; Zanga cites the Albanian news agency, ATA, dispatch of June 23, 1986.

66. Within months after Hoxha's death, the USSR began a concerted effort, through signals in Soviet media coverage of Albania and in broadcasts to Albania, to demonstrate that there were advantages to be found in renewed ties with the "socialist commonwealth." For example, see various Soviet broadcasts and articles in principal Soviet newspapers cited in FBIS, *Daily Report, Soviet Union* (May 17, 1985, pp. F13–14 and May 30, 1985, pp. F1–2).

67. Nelson, *Alliance Behavior in the Warsaw Pact,* especially pp. 71–107.

68. Peter Bender, *East Europe in Search of Security* (Baltimore, Md.: The Johns Hopkins University Press, 1972), p. 104.

69. Author's adaptation from Anthanassios G. Platias and R.J. Rydell, "International Security Regimes: The Case of a Balkan Nuclear Free Zone," in Carlton and Schaerf, eds., *South-Eastern Europe After Tito,* p. 118.

70. Daniel N. Nelson, "The Romanian Disaster," in T. Anthony Jones, ed., *Research on the Soviet Union and Eastern Europe* (Cambridge, Mass.: JAI Press, 1990).

71. Bender, *East Europe in Search of Security,* p. 102.

2

The Yugoslav Precipice

The disintegration of Yugoslavia, precipitated by civil war, is no longer unthinkable. Slovene and Croatian separatism, Albanian demands in Kosovo, and the rise of Serbian nationalism against these targets, may be the impetus for such a disaster. The West waited far too long to recognize impending trouble in Yugoslavia, and has offered far too little economic and political support with which tangible strengths in this complex state might have been built upon. How did Yugoslavia reach this precipice? What can the West do?

Federalism to Confederalism to Nationalism

Seventy years ago, President Woodrow Wilson's Fourteen Points forcefully enunciated the principle of self-determination. At the Versailles Peace Conference, Wilson insisted on the creation of a Yugoslav state from the remnants of the Austro-Hungarian empire, plus the Slavic Kingdoms that had broken from the Ottomans in 1877–1878 (Serbia and Montenegro).[1] Since Tito's death in 1980, that Wilsonian image of a union among Southeast European Slavs has been first shaken by incremental confederalism, and is now all but discarded.

Formally, Yugoslavia is a federal state of six national republics and two large autonomous provinces within Serbia, the biggest republic. Those two autonomous provinces—Vojvodina and Kosovo—had the status of republics in many respects based upon the 1974 Constitution. Further, Yugoslavia's twenty-four million people are divided among diverse nations, with religious and language differences reinforcing nationality distinctions.[2] Catholic, Protestant and Orthodox Christians mix with millions of Moslems while the Serbo-Croatian language is ignored in the republics of Slovenia in the north and Macedonia in the south, and Albanian is spreading with the rapid growth of that minority.

But these well-known cleavages within Yugoslavia are not what accelerated incremental confederalism and nationalist reactions. Rather, the

35

demise of federalism came at the hands of weak central leadership, confronting economic failure and ethnic tensions. Virtually guaranteed by the 1974 Constitution, and fathered by the principal Yugoslav leader of the century, Josef Broz Tito, such weak leadership cannot be escaped within current institutional arrangements—except, that is, by seeking to destroy those institutions through demagogic appeals. Tito, who had led the Partisan guerrilla army against Nazi occupiers and who had single-handedly split from Stalin in 1948 to lead Yugoslavia on a non-aligned course, no doubt understood fully that he alone symbolized unity that transcended national and regional rivalries. Lacking an heir with similar charisma or stature, institutions necessarily must incorporate diverse interests and assuage fears, rather that override them. Having effected purges to oust Croatian nationalism from the League of Communists of Yugoslavia (LCY, the League or the Party) in 1971,[3] Tito commissioned a document designed to avoid such nationalistic challenges after his death.

Tito could not have foreseen, however, the degree to which that document has, a decade after his death, de-federalized the entire state bureaucracy and even the League. Each republic has its own party organization, republican presidency and assembly, while the Federal Presidency requires rotation for one year terms among republics, and the presidency of the party presidium has de facto rotation although it is not mandated. As a result, the Federal President until May 1990, Janez Drnovsek (who is Slovene), and Milan Pancevski, who was then president of the League of Yugoslav Communists Central Committee Presidium (i.e., party leader), had little international stature and little power vis-à-vis each constituent Yugoslav republic. Drnovsek is young, articulate, and trained in economics (a Ph.D on IMF relations with Yugoslavia). He does not have, however, any international recognition or widespread political power outside Slovenia. Borisav Jovic, who became federal president on May 15, 1990 when Drnovsek's term expired, is not trusted by Milosevic, and one can anticipate heightened tensions between Serbia and the weak federal institutions. The federal prime minister, now Ante Markovic, replaced Branko Mukulic in January 1989 after the latter's resignation. The prime minister has a four-year term—but no policy decision can be taken without virtually unanimous approval among republics.

The dilemma of federal leadership has had deleterious consequences for systemic reform. Because the Party and State have had such weak central authority after Tito's death, greater pluralism was feared as a harbinger of an uncontrollable centrifugal momentum. Such a fear contributed to bureaucratic inertia that overrode countless studies pointing to the need for fundamental restructuring. The state/party bureaucracy grew in strength as the central leadership was unable to build any political base from which to challenge existing interests. There were many steps that allegedly deepened "self-management" and "delegational representation," but few measures did anything substantive. Everyone, it seems, has for some time understood Yugoslavia's systemic problems, ranging from ethno-nationalist conflicts, overbureaucratization, the League's stranglehold on appointments etc., but no one had the political power to step forward and act.

The absence of central leadership is understood painfully throughout Yugoslavia, but there are no clear solutions. A study produced by the State Presidency in February 1987 recommended no fewer than 130 changes in the 1974 Constitution. Prolonged debate about these recommendations led the Federal Assembly to adapt 39 amendments to the Constitution in November 1988, most of which focused on economic decentralization and deregulation. The 1963 Constitution is viewed as attractive by some insofar as a united Yugoslavia was emphasized in that document—but it was that stress on central government which produced suspicion in most republics outside of Serbia.

Serbian criticism of the 1974 Constitution has been particularly vehement, and differs in substance from legal or scholarly assessments of that document. Slobodan Milosevic argues that the 1974 Constitution is destroying the country, especially because it stipulates that executive power is rotated, thereby diluting leadership.[4] By contrast, academic studies tend to emphasize the economic effects of the Constitution, and are highly critical of continued state ownership and central planning while political pluralism is denied.[5]

The peculiar crisis of Yugoslavia thus finds the existence of a Yugoslav state threatened and the institutions of that state—including the League of Yugoslav Communists—disintegrating. Put another way, the federal party bureaucracy and leadership have been made less and less relevant to political outcomes in Yugoslavia.

Still highly relevant, however, are the republican parties where hard-fought political battles are won and lost. The 1987 victory of Slobodan ("Slobo") Milosevic in a struggle for the Serbian party's chairmanship defeating the Belgrade party chief signaled not only how far nationalism had penetrated the League, but also how completely separate parties pursuing quite distinct paths have emerged. Meanwhile, of course, Slovenian, Croatian and other communist and opposition parties have seen Milosevic's leadership of the Serbian communist party as threatening. Milosevic's leadership tactics have been dangerously populist in the sense of fomenting through rhetoric (and perhaps through direct organizational efforts) mass demonstrations against the Albanian majority in Kosovo, against leadership in Vojvodina and Montenegro (both of which resigned *en masse* in October 1988 and January 1989, respectively), and for constitutional amendments which deny much of the autonomy of Kosovo and Vojvodina. But the same tactics also have pushed the Slovenes and Croatians away much more rapidly than would have otherwise been the case.

After two years of rhetorical jousting, the Slovenes took dramatic steps in early 1990 to break away from Yugoslavia. First, Slovene communists detached themselves from the League of Yugoslav Communists and then, when campaigning began for April 1990 elections in the republic, it became clear that public sympathies had moved towards complete independence. An electoral triumph by the "Demos" (Democratic Opposition of Slovenia) brought to power a national-conservative orientation led by the Slovene Democratic Alliance. Pushed by Milosevic's fiery statements and resurgent Serbian nationalism, Slovenes "see themselves as bullied by outside authorities, their economic interests trampled [and their] ethnic pride hurt."[6] As a consequence, polls suggest that the political winds will continue to blow strongly towards secession from Yugoslavia, unless the new constitution enables Slovenia to be only loosely associated with Yugoslav confederation.

Indeed, during the latter half of 1990, a new constitution for the Republic of Slovenia, clearly outlining its sovereignty, was proposed by Milan Kucan (Slovene president). On July 2, 1990, the Slovene Assembly adopted a proclamation of sovereignty that incorporated those sentiments. The Federal Presidency in Belgrade responded by calling on the Slovenes to suspend their declaration. By late 1990, this issue was still unresolved, although the Yugoslav People's Army had, on orders from the Federal Presidency, taken steps to deny to Slovenia any arms to form a territorial defense force loyal to local authorities.

Croatian-Serbian antagonisms also worsened in 1990. Croatian elections in early 1990 led to the victory of conservatives and nationalists, especially the Croatian Democratic Union. That party's leader, Franjo Tudjman, became Croatia's president. In June, he advocated a new Croatian constitution that the republic's Serbian minority interpreted as a threat. Headed by Jovan Raskovic, leader of the Serb Democratic Party of Knin, the municipalities of Croatia in which Serbs constitute a majority rejected (in early July) proposed changes in the republic's constitution. About 600,000 of Croatia's five million people are Serbs and, although the nationalities live side by side in many urban areas, Serbian nationalism is potent in districts such as Knin where the Serb population is concentrated. In late July, an Association of Serbs from Croatia was formed, holding its inaugural meeting in Belgrade, with Jovan Raskovic as its chairman. There is a widespread view that Milosevic, by hosting such a meeting and other actions, exhibits a desire to exploit unrest in Croatia. August and September of 1990 saw sometimes violent confrontations,

The Yugoslav Precipice

particularly in and around Knin, as Serbs blockaded roads, and fired on Croatian police sent to quell demonstrations and to end the disruption of transportation and commerce. Barricades were later reinforced and, in 1991, further clashes between the Knin Serbs and either Croatian police or the Federal army are quite possible.

At the same time, Milosevic is seeking to dominate Yugoslav political life—or, at least, politics in all republics except Slovenia and Croatia—via the tactics of mass unrest. His pointed attacks on bureaucracy and vague references to saving Yugoslavia, imply an authoritarian nationalism in populist clothing. At once the object of fear and adulation, Milosevic has the potential to become an archetypical "autocratic populist"—a cult figure.[7] Exploiting Serbian nationalism, Milosevic has built a foundation for his political power across regions and even republics, rooted among ethnic Serbs. Rallies of hundreds of thousands in Belgrade and among Serbs in Croatia make his popularity clear, and his potential demagogic effect quite tangible.

Whether or not Milosevic will succeed in his quest to be another Tito is doubtful. Certainly, he lacks the legitimacy of a wartime leader, and has capitalized only on pre-existing issues to mobilize Serbs. His effort to oust Stipe Suvar from the post of president of the party's politburo in an early February 1989 central committee plenum failed—although Milosevic's demand for an immediate extraordinary party congress was, in part, approved (the congress was held in late January 1990, a half year earlier than scheduled). The congress, however, did not go Milosevic's way, ending in chaos rather than with a triumphant Serbian leader. When the congress adjourned on January 23, 1990, a Yugoslav party on which Milosevic might have thought he could build his leadership was shattered, the Slovene delegation having walked out. It is also possible, although far from certain, that Ante Markovic, the current federal prime minister, will succeed where others have failed abysmally—slowing inflation and stimulating renewed confidence in central leadership. Markovic, whose background includes an admirable record as director of Croatia's largest enterprise, may have the skills and savvy for the task, but (of course) the task may be overwhelming in scope.

The Yugoslav People's Army (JNA) plays a large role, as well, in the country's leadership uncertainties. Top officers are clearly troubled not only by ethnic unrest (to which I will return) but also by what Rear Admiral and Deputy Defense Minister Stane Brovet called "political disunity" that can lead to a national "catastrophe."[8] When even the party's President, Stipe Suvar, admitted in February 1989 that the party is "incapable of making historical decisions" and that "all [the party does] is grope in the dark," the military must see itself as the only remaining institution with a capacity for action to save the country.

That the military has become more frightened about prospects for a political collapse, and more determined to prevent the dissolution of Yugoslavia, is evident in the comments made by leading officers in late 1989. Whereas there is a seemingly sincere commitment to accept democratic evolution, the army does not view positively Milosevic's inflammatory rhetoric and related "nationalist passions." Deputy Defense Minister Simeon Buncic was adamant in mid to late 1989 that the army sees the capacity of federal institutions as necessary for social stability.[9] The army, in short, does not like, and may see the need to counter, both the nationalist extremes of Milosevic and the efforts by other republics (notably Slovenia) to weaken federal authority. At the same time, no Serbian officer could be sanguine about trying to operate in hostile environments throughout Yugoslavia with conscripts drawn from all regions and nationalities.[10]

Economic Paralysis

Yugoslav political unraveling was accelerated by a mounting economic paralysis in the 1980s, made worse when compared with the country's economic growth of the 1950s–1960s (above 9% per year on average). Although foreseen for many years, the 1980s made it dramatically clear that Yugoslav political difficulties inextricably are intertwined with vicious economic problems inherited from the economic halfway house of market socialism.[11] Analyses by IMF and Yugoslavia's own economists reveal that there remains far too much bureaucratic interference, state ownership, and limits on international trade to spur productivity and innovation; conversely, Tito long ago reversed the Yugoslav imitation of a Stalinist economy. One thus finds an economy straining against itself, unable to shake loose from residual elements of state socialism, while also being psychologically unwilling to impose stringent central controls. Instead, the Mikulic government opted to combat economic problems by tinkering with the "consensual economy" (*dogovorna ekonomija*) that has long served as the ersatz market socialism of Yugoslavia.

During the two and a half years of the Mikulic government, inflation rose from 90% to 200% annually and became devastating for Yugoslavs who must live on fixed incomes. Even government data indicated a 24% decline in real wages in 1988. In 1989, inflation continued its upward spiral to an annual rate that some say exceeded 2,000%, while over one and a quarter million (15% of the work force) were unemployed in late 1989.[12] Living standards are, by most estimates, regressing towards 1960 levels. At the same time, inequalities of several kinds are worsening. Regional income differences have been increasing constantly since the

1950s. Additionally, inequalities at the workplace, due to category, position and education (all affected by League membership) have worsened.

The network of privileges that determines access to housing, goods and services as well as job placement, affects all of Yugoslav society. The economic picture is worse, however, for certain strata of society, and has been reinforced by the political inequality administered by and for League of Communist members.[13]

Thus far, Yugoslavia has been unable to compete successfully in the world market, using credit to import more than it can hope to pay for. After debt reached about $21 billion, climbing during the 1980s because of unpaid principal, some modest turnaround was achieved in 1989. Foreign debt, however, is a severe problem insofar as servicing it requires a huge proportion of export earning. Some parts of Yugoslavia, especially Slovenia, do not have these dire economic conditions except insofar Slovenes need the larger Yugoslav market and raw materials. But Slovenes point to their disproportionally large share of the Yugoslav GNP (almost 20%) and of Yugoslav exports (24%), suggesting that other republics could learn from their example.

It is no wonder that the European Community (EC) has been very reluctant to seriously consider Yugoslav entry, since the subsidization of Yugoslavia's non-competitive industry and agriculture would cost the Community a great deal. Yet, one may speculate whether or not civil war and a million refugees from a Yugoslavia ignited in ethnic and labor violence would be a cheaper alternative than assuming large economic burdens dispersed throughout the European Community.

Earnest discussions, and often heated debates, occur frequently regarding the Yugoslav economy. The well-respected Zagreb economist, Professor Stavko Kulic, has articulated a position, held more widely as time goes on, that wrong premises have guided economic policies; development and growth do not come from imported technology that spurs large-scale industry. Rather, Kulic says, Yugoslavia's inability to prosper is a direct consequence of its own lack of expertise and technology. It follows that imports to generate export-led growth should be substituted by an effort to develop domestic strengths and expertise, to rely more on Yugoslavia's own resources and innovations, and export that which can be supported only by indigenous talents.

It is, in all probability, too late for such a wholesale reversal. Prime Minister Ante Markovic's economic reform package has, in fact, run into resolute opposition from Slobodan Milosevic and his allies in Montenegro, including huge anti-austerity protests in Belgrade and elsewhere in Serbia, with unenthusiastic endorsement from politicians in other republics. Since the Markovic plan did not require that all republics support the proposal in the Federal Assembly (a ⅔ majority *is* necessary, however), most of its provisions became law at the outset of 1990. Most notable, and controversial, among Markovic's emergency measures are steps meant to attack the country's hyperinflation including a wage freeze for half a year, withdrawing state subsidies for enterprises that show no profit, the drastic devaluation of the dinar, and the introduction of a convertible dinar by tying the currency to the West German mark.[14] Given the extent of public and political opposition to these measures in Serbia, dramatized throughout extensive fall 1989 strikes by Serbian workers who protested both inflation and the idea of a wage freeze to combat it, Markovic's plan is unlikely to be a permanent solution. Inflation *did* subside greatly in early 1990, but the system's structural flaws remain. The longer inflation remains lower, however, the better chance Markovic will have of confronting structural dilemmas.

One major obstacle preventing structural remedies is the endemic corruption among Yugoslav enterprises and their financing. In mid-1987, world-wide attention was drawn to the scandal that originated in the 29th largest enterprise in all of Yugoslavia—the Bosnian firm Agrokomerc.[15] This twenty-five year-old firm had expanded widely in the Yugoslav economy, from its original base in agriculture and forestry, to industrial and mining operations. The top executives of Agrokomerc, with the tolerance of many people in high political positions in that republic (Bosnia-Herzogovina, with its capital of Sarajevo), "balanced" their books through promissory notes (bills of exchange or IOUs) issued to banks throughout Yugoslavia *without collateral*. Such promises to pay later were accepted by banks because of non-existent check-ups, because they dared not question such an important and well-backed operation, *and* because the procedure is widespread and flagrant in Yugoslavia.

When it was discovered that Agrokomerc had obtained several hundred million dollars (the exact amount may never be known) through such unsecured promissory notes, heads began to roll. Fikret Abdic, Chairman of the Board of Agrokomerc, and member of the Bosnian Party Central Committee, was arrested and jailed. By the fall of 1987, most of the other top Agrokomerc people were behind bars, and Yugoslav newspapers and news magazines began to refer to the episode as "Agrogate." The scandal also forced the resignation of Hamdija Pozderac from the collective State Presidency where he was serving as vice president. He further resigned from his post in the Republican Central Committee.

The Agrokomerc scandal is now old news in Yugoslavia. Trials of principal figures in 1988 failed to renew the same outrage as when first revealed, and today few heads turn when the scandal is mentioned. Yet, the implications of such revelations are unequivocal—enterprise directors and managers, particularly outside the wealthier republics of Slovenia and Croatia, cannot balance their books legitimately. The combination of a subsidized living standard for employees—in a sense, paying people for more than their productivity warrants—with undependable domestic supplies and uncertain foreign markets have furthered an already potent Balkan tendency towards' dishonest management. That scores of people have been indicted or administratively punished due to Agrokomerc will have little lasting effect on this endemic problem. And, insofar as Slovenia and Croatia see Agrokomerc as an example of Bosnian and "southern" corruption and waste, the scandal gives greater impetus to confederalism. Informed observers of Yugoslavia know well, of course, that Croatian and Slovenian firms (e.g., INA, the Croatian oil firm) engage in the same practices that led to the fall of a Bosnian conglomerate.

Potent Nationalism

The greatest danger to Yugoslavia's existence is the ever-potent sentiment of ethno-nationalism. Nowhere is the conflict among Yugoslav nationalisms more volatile than in Kosovo. Slovene and Croatian separatism, and Serbian reactions to both, were mentioned earlier. But the Kosovo issue has, perhaps, the greatest potential to ignite civil war.

To be sure, no one knows with precision the component values or behavior of nationalism. Yet, when people of one ethno-linguistic group, largely distinguished as well by religion, exhibit heightened identity and solidarity with that group, and demonstrate a willingness to sacrifice for their ethno-linguistic population, nationalism is no doubt an appropriate descriptive term. In Yugoslavia, there are many "nationalisms," some growing in reaction to others. In the late 1960s and early 1970s, Croatian nationalists resorted to international terrorism to promote their cause. Their counterproductive strategy resulted in worldwide condemnation, and a severe crackdown by Tito.[16]

In the early 1980s, the most vocal and active nationalism was among Albanians in the autonomous province within Serbia called Kosovo. Albanians had long been in Kosovo, which borders on Albania. During the lengthy regime of Enver Hoxha in Albania, some Albanians fled to Kosovo. Yet most of Kosovo's rapidly increasing Albanian population has been the consequence of their very high birth rate. Forty years ago a minority in Kosovo, Albanians now constitute 90% (1.8 million) of the province's population. Although it would be a mistake to assume that ethnic Albanians are of one mind in their relations with Belgrade and the Yugoslav federation—cleavages exist, for example, between Albanians with jobs versus the 40% who are unemployed, between Moslems and Christians, etc.—it is nevertheless true that an Albanian separatist movement has wide support in Kosovo. In April 1981, riots in Pristina (the largest city in Kosovo), particular at the University of Pristina, threatened civil authority in that province. The League viewed the events as sufficiently dangerous to necessitate military intervention. Almost 25% of JNA was dispatched to Kosovo and, although that force was gradually withdrawn, the memory of 1981 events remained fresh for both sides. In October 1987, an additional 400-man federal police unit was sent into Kosovo as tensions again rose.

Then, in February 1989, martial law and regular JNA troops returned after Albanian strikes among miners and protests mounted against constitutional changes that lessen Kosovo's autonomy. Reports of "armored columns dug in with camouflage protection," of an armored regiment camped in a field between Pristina and Titova Mitrovica, and of "infantry brigades . . . marching towards Pec" make it clear that an armed uprising is ongoing. In the last week of March 1989, scores died in fighting between Albanians and riot police or army units. Young Albanians, some armed with pistols and automatic weapons, ambushed military units or sniped at them from buildings on city streets.

In early 1990, the antagonisms between Albanians and Serbs concerning Kosovo's status burst into the open again with tragic results. Martial law was renewed and thousands of troops were again moved into the region. Violent confrontations in February left dozens dead, and armed contingents of Serbs from neighboring areas were reported to have been formed to defend against Albanian "atrocities." Milosevic used these events to underscore his dissatisfaction with federal authorities' handling of the situation, and to lodge his most vituperative attacks yet on Markovic and against the leadership of other republics.[17] In the aftermath of these clashes, which added to deaths in 1989 meant that more than 60 people had been killed in Kosovo's ethnic violence, Serbia suspended the parliament and government in Pristina. This early July 1990 action was resisted by Albanian deputies in the Kosovo parliament who, in September, met clandestinely to adopt an alternative constitution. But neither this action, nor continuing deadly violence, seems likely to dissuade Serbia leaders from reintegrating the province into Serbia—and, as that effort continues, Albanians will react with protests and strikes, followed by vicious clashes with police. The prognosis is poor, indeed.

For Serbians, Albanians represent a national threat. For Slovenes and Croats, Albanians are an economic drain and are seen as a cultural backwater (alongside Macedonia and Montenegro). Even such a respected academic as the Director of the Economic Institute in Zagreb, Croatia, Branko Horvat, has criticized the low preparation of Albanian students from the University of Pristina, especially in technological sciences.

Serbian nationalism is a core element of Slobodan Milosevic's appeal, with the most immediate object of vilification being Albanians. It is, for Serbs, not only that the Albanians have procreated themselves into a

The Yugoslav Precipice

majority (in the Serb's view), but that the historical roots of Serbs in Kosovo are being wiped out. Serbian rights within Kosovo are one of Milosevic's principal appeals to mass sentiments. Although it would be a mistake to attribute the "Slobo" phenomenon to ethno-nationalism alone—there is a strong anti-bureaucratic element embedded in his charisma as well—the core ingredient is undoubtedly Serbs versus Albanians, Slovenes, Croats and others.

In late June 1987, the League of Communist's Central Committee debated fifty-eight proposals about "stabilizing" the Kosovo situation, and adopted almost two dozen. It was hoped that the steps, which were both socioeconomic and procedural, would defuse the Serbian and Albanian nationalisms that were on a collision course, and to mitigate the appeal of separatists.

But this optimal scenario was never likely. Instead, evidence that cooler heads were not prevailing was apparent almost immediately after the "stabilization" proposals were enacted. In the Serbian town of Paracin in early September 1987, an Albanian conscript in the JNA shot and killed four of his fellow soldiers—Serbs, Croats and Muslims—and then killed himself. A note indicating his separatist feelings was, apparently, left by the young recruit. The "Paracin Massacre," as it was dubbed, was shocking to Serbs and to the military high command which has sought carefully to find and eliminate separatist cells within the JNA.

It was in the aftermath of this event that, on September 23, 1987, then Defense Minister Branko Mamula was quoted in the military journal *Naroda Armija* as having said at an army conference that social problems were threatening the country and that the Party was being ignored.[18] Mamula, supported by General Georgije Jovocic, the JNA's party chief, was firing a warning shot across the bow, so to speak, of civilian authorities. Shortly thereafter, rumors that there were officers in the army who had plans for a coup were denied by official sources.[19]

The army is the only Yugoslav institution that remains intact, and its chief officers blame politicians and the media for endangering the country. The Party has now split into many parties, and socioeconomic institutions have devolved to republic-level control. Given the origins of a post-war communist Yugoslavia in Tito's Partisans, it is fair to say that the army and the party were once indistinguishable. As Partisan veterans have aged, retired and died, the party and JNA have become increasingly distinct from each other and, some might say, alien to each other. At the very least, Mamula's concerns reflect beliefs of the JNA officer corp that the federal state it is to defend (e.g., against the Soviets, Bulgarians or other invaders) is coming unraveled, and pulling the army down the same path. The army, unequivocally, opposes the multiplicity of narrow republican interests, and fears that national fragmentation threatens "the elementary order which must exist in every state. . . ."[20]

Military intervention is now plausible, but not yet highly probable. The violence in Kosovo, with the army once again involved in de facto combat within Yugoslavia, is only one of the conditions that contribute to the heightened potential for army action. If other multi-ethnic regions such as Bosnia, parts of Croatia or Montenegro also disintegrate into organized violence by one group against another, the army's resources would be stretched beyond capacity if called into each area.

Further enhancing the likelihood of military intervention would be the action of Slovenia or Croatia to break away from the Yugoslav federation. Already, Slovene communists have separated from the League, and Slovenia has accepted multi-party pluralism, and a non-communist government has been elected. Were forces antithetical to socialism to take control in Ljubljana and/or Zagreb, the army's commitment to a Yugoslav state would be fundamentally tested. By October 1989, it was already rumored in Belgrade that President Drnovsek had relieved several top ethnic Serbian officers of their commands because of suspicion that a pro-Milosevic plot was developing, aimed at resolving the country's crisis by imposing strong central government from Serbia.[21]

That the Army would act at the behest of the Federal Presidency to assert central authority, however, was made clear in late September and early October 1990 as the Fifth Army Area Command was ordered to take control of weapons, material and transport assets stored in depots for the territorial defense forces of Slovenia. Constitutional changes passed by the Slovene Assembly on September 27–28 made it clear that a territorial army, loyal only to the Slovene government, was to be formed, armed with weapons and equipment heretofore earmarked for an "all people's defense" of Yugoslavia. By the first days of October, the JNA was moving equipment and weapons out of the republic, while maintaining control of the depots themselves.

JNA general officers were all aware that threats confronting the military were internal, and blame politicians and the media—especially in Slovenia and Croatia—for failing to realize that catastrophe looms ahead.[22] Slovene politicians, media and youth groups have carried on a running battle with the JNA, and the attacks on Admiral Mamula, other leading officers and military institutions generally, have precipitated highly negative responses from the army. The JNA is far from being enamored with the Croatian political atmosphere either.[23]

From all this, Yugoslavia would appear to be engaged in a kind of self-induced entropy, with little chance to avoid worst-case scenarios such as a cycle of mass civil unrest, and military intervention.

Yugoslav Strengths

Yet, this is a Yugoslav sort of crisis in that none of the conditions described above, and perhaps not even all of them together, preordain the demise of a loosely defined Yugoslav state. There are, indeed substantial strengths upon which Yugoslavs can rely, and rebuild.

Foremost among these positive factors is the still widely-shared commitment to a democratic and pluralistic polity, in which there is ample freedom for political, social and economic debate. Academics, journalists and party members advocate, very openly, almost any position (a view that has now been accepted in principle by all republics' party organizations, but with the Slovenes going much further). The Serbian weekly *Nin*, akin to *Time Magazine*, was, prior to Milosevic, often daring and sometimes wrong (e.g., when it printed a World War II photo of three young boys in Nazi uniforms, and identified them as the "Brothers Dizdarevic," implying that the then-Foreign Minister Raif Dizdarevic may have been in the photo).

Yet, *Nin, Politika* (Belgrade), *Borba* (the daily of the Socialist alliance), *Vjesnik* in Zagreb or *Dnevnik* and *Delo* in Ljubljana—not to mention regional publications and scholarly books—stake out wide parts of the political spectrum. Although *Nin* and *Politika* have become mouthpieces of Milosevic since his selection as Serbian party leader, they are not fully "controlled" and conservatives must be wary of the press.

This Yugoslav "glasnost" is not new. Such a strength should not be underestimated, both as a safety-valve and as a genuine forum for the development of alternative strategies while uncovering systemic problems. Milosevic has already criticized the open press, forced resignations and curtailed funds—but the press and other media are too diverse to be controlled from Serbia alone, even if Milosevic remains in control of the republic. In Slovenia, the journal of the Socialist Youth Alliance, *Mladina*, has been unrelenting in its criticism of the army and in its markedly pro-Albanian stance regarding Kosovo. But, by 1990 *Mladina* is only one voice among scores of radical publications active throughout Slovenia and Croatia.

Within the commitment to an open society is a broad consensus that Yugoslavia requires a federal system, with significant limits on central authority coupled with effective central institutions in matters of economic, social, and defense policy. This consensus is not very specific, and is precarious in Slovenia. Nevertheless, few advocates of secession from a federal Yugoslav state are sanguine about economic prospects or security for smaller and weaker republics trying to make it on their own.

Further, it is undeniable that Yugoslavia's decades of nonalignment— Tito having been with Nasser and Nehru the architects of that movement—

is a positive element for the future. Reputationally, Americans and West Europeans still recall with respect Tito's break from Stalin in 1948, and are inclined to support Yugoslavia's course to the extent that Yugoslav actions do not conflict with Western interests. It may not be that nonalignment brought economic benefit to Yugoslavia—indeed, the country's largesse to "Third World" students meant significant cost to a state that was rather poor itself by European standards. Nevertheless, there is a reservoir of good will that Yugoslavia may use to its benefit.

Yugoslavia's links to Western Europe's competitive democracies, and its desire to enter Europe further, also reinforce those who seek further to democratize Yugoslav politics and to accelerate economic reforms that would strengthen the market mechanisms in the economy. Indeed, there is wide agreement in the intelligentsia that greater democracy and an enhanced role for free market principles should be sought—although that consensus breaks down when specific matters of political procedure and resource allocation are discussed. However, there is far less disagreement in Yugoslavia about *where* to go than about how to get there.

We should also note that some republics, especially Slovenia, continue to do extremely well in economic terms. Notwithstanding the economic trauma that very high hard-currency debt and triple-digit inflation implies, Slovenes have negligible unemployment (as opposed to a Yugoslav average of 15%, and a level in Kosovo of 40%), and a very high standard of living. Slovenia needs all of Yugoslavia as a market, however, since (despite what Slovenes might want to think about making their republic into a small Switzerland) the republic's products are not on the whole competitive in the advanced European countries. There are reasons to expect that Ljubljana wants more than its own prosperity; after all, higher employment elsewhere means a shrinking domestic market. There is, then, economic health in the midst of economic hardship—a well-being that continues to be evident in most of Yugoslavia's cities outside of Macedonia, Montenegro and Kosovo (i.e., the underdeveloped south).

There *are* dangerous trends and conditions in this important and multifaceted state. It is adrift with no discernible Yugoslav leadership, while the ominous signs of powerful and disruptive nationalisms have grown strong enough that violent episodes have now begun anew with little chance to be extinguished without more bloodshed. Further, the Yugoslav mid-way course of economic policy had long ago run out of steam, and required an injection of new reform. Markovic's program of economic reform, however, is more likely in the short run to *exacerbate* an already bad unemployment figure while it lowers inflation, which will fuel the already virulent nationalisms. The army's concerns about Kosovo and the socioeconomic condition of Yugoslavia are, themselves, of concern insofar as it connotes impatience mixed with fear. Its troops have been in combat in Kosovo, and the JNA must find its role to be highly discomfiting.

Yet, it would be erroneous to expect confidently the utter demise of Yugoslavia, for almost no citizen or public figure in any republic—Albanian separatists aside—*wants* that outcome. For such an outcome would yield a group of small, weak states without the economic or political wherewithal to be more than the military clients of superpowers or the appendages to a German "Mitteleuropa." With each other, there remains the potential to avoid the fate this area of Southeast Europe knew all too well before World War I, and which Tito avoided in 1948.

Yugoslavia *is* a system under grave duress, needing leadership and fundamental reform in political and economic realms. But Yugoslavia is also a state with a *raison d'être* for its constituent republics and peoples, and some tangible strengths that reinforce its unity. This is a period of a Yugoslav kind of crisis, but one for which a catastrophe is not the only, or assured, outcome.

Implications for Western Policy

As reports of ethnic violence mount, while the fight against inflation may mean higher unemployment that contributes to the dangerous nationalism of Serbian leader Slobodan Milosevic, members of the European Community and NATO have substantial interests in Yugoslavia's future. We bear some historical responsibility for the emergence of such a state in Southeastern Europe, dating back to the Versailles Conference. Forty years ago, as well, the West applauded and supported Tito's departure from Soviet tutelage, hoping that other "satellite" states would follow Yugoslav non-alignment and self-management—the calling-cards of Tito's long rule.[24]

The fading of Yugoslavia's prominence in Western foreign policy priorities, however, has been evident in tangible respects. By the mid-1980s, for example, Yugoslavia ceased to be a net recipient of developmental assistance from the West according to World Bank data, although it was at a time when inflation, unemployment and debt were mounting rapidly. And, whereas in the 1950s and 1960s the United States was the principal provider of weapons for the Yugoslav ground and air forces, the USSR became the main source of arms transfers (roughly $500 million from 1982–1987 versus just over $100 million from the U.S.), and began to provide the Mig-25 air superiority fighter for Yugoslavia's air force.[25] The Soviets also stepped in during the early 1980s to enlarge its trading role with Yugoslavia; by 1980 over 40% of Yugoslavia's trade was with CMEA states, and the USSR was the largest single trading partner. In the late 1980s, Yugoslav trade swung towards Western Europe (particularly West Germany),[26] although over a quarter of Yugoslav imports and exports remain with CMEA members.

Why Western emphasis came to be placed elsewhere in Eastern and Southeastern Europe by the 1970s is not difficult to see. On the one hand, Ceausescu's Romania seemed to offer (before human rights violations and a bizarre familial cult negated any benefit Romania provided) an opportunity to enhance diversity within the Soviet "bloc," while other crises in Czechoslovakia and Poland captured NATO's attention. At the same time, the waning of bipolarity and the emergence of Japan, China, the EC and other powerful actors in world politics made Yugoslavia's role as a non-aligned leader less critical as a bridge between East and West. Other leaders from whom the non-aligned movement originated— Nehru, Nasser, and Sukarno—have had transient legacies insofar as India, Egypt, and Indonesia have all become associated with the U.S. or USSR. Being part of neither bloc had distinct advantages for Yugoslavia, but it added little—especially in the 1970s and 1980s—to West European or American attention.

Domestically, too, Yugoslavia's vaunted self-management experiment ossified, and strikes became common during the 1980s. This labor unrest, and obvious political, social and economic problems, make Yugoslav socialism less attractive for poorer countries to emulate or for the most developed states to underwrite. French and West German governments were among the principal lenders to Yugoslavia in the 1970s, but did little in the 1980s. For American commercial banks, which have by far the largest share of outstanding U.S. loans to Yugoslavia, the notion of additional loans or credits has been unattractive. Meanwhile, the Reagan and Bush Administrations, despite support from the Export-Import Bank and the Commodity Credit Corporation in earlier presidencies, gave Yugoslavia's IMF-guided stabilization program rhetorical commendation and promises of "constructive assistance," but no new financial aid. Americans did participate in renegotiations of Yugoslav debt in the late 1980s, easing payment schedules. New lines of credit, however, are thus far slow to open. Further negotiations were conducted in 1988 and 1989, but produced few concrete results.

Sometimes, of course, specific policies of the Yugoslav government have caused difficulties from the Western standpoint. For example, Yugoslav support for the PLO and radical Arab states (exhibited during the 1973 October War and in 1982 when Soviet aircraft were allowed transit through Yugoslavia), and unwillingness to make strenuous efforts to combat terrorism, have not been received warmly by NATO. When the Yugoslavs failed in 1985 to extradite Abdul Abbas, who planned the

The Yugoslav Precipice 51

"Achille Lauro" hijacking, a low-point was reached in Washington's view of Belgrade.

The distance between Belgrade and the West thus has many origins. Yet none are insurmountable. From the Yugoslav side, diminished inclination to align Yugoslavia with presumed interests of the "Third World" has been evident in the late 1980s. At the same time greater attention has been given to issues more germane to their own immediate security in the Balkans, and new non-communist or coalition governments in Hungary, Romania and Bulgaria are receiving many economic and diplomatic delegations from Belgrade and vice versa.

An effective Western diplomacy presupposes that our knowledge of Yugoslav reality is informed by detailed information from the republic and provincial level, as well as thorough assessments of issues as seen from Belgrade. On the international plane, Yugoslavia's debt, lack of new Western credits and economic or military ties to the Soviet Union should not, in and of themselves, dissuade EC or NATO governments from efforts to assist Yugoslavs. We ought not, as well, assume that forty years of non-alignment will be set aside on issues such as the Arab-Israeli conflict.

Finally, of course, we should reject the view that the demise of a unified Yugoslavia is already preordained. Western impatience with the absence of strong federal leadership is not shared by elites in the various republics and provinces, and a military coup is not thought to be a certain outcome of current ethnic violence.

That Yugoslavia confronts a precipice with its own survival in the balance is well understood. But, since that state has not yet collapsed, and since the West has ample reason to hope that it does not, we should see clearly that our best interests lie with rapid reform generated by responsible leaders. Helping Prime Minister Ante Markovic with new credits/grants, or relief from debt incurred in the 1970s, would have salutary effects and could diminish the appeal of Serbian nationalist, Slobodan Milosevic. When Markovic visited Washington in October 1989, for example, the American response was largely non-committal and carried little new economic assistance. Providing greater diplomatic visibility and recognition for Markovic and a unified Yugoslavia would also be appropriate. The possibility of creating an international peace-keeping force for deployment in Kosovo may be a way in which to defuse escalating violence, and should be explored by the West via CSCE.

The West cannot manufacture a survival plan for Yugoslavia, but it must see its compelling interests that require immediate and substantial investments in a looser but federal and democratic Yugoslav state. We had a role in Yugoslavia's creation; let us not ignore that historical tie and thereby watch Yugoslavia slip over the precipice.

Notes

1. Ivo J. Lederer, *Yugoslavia at the Paris Peace Conference* (New Haven: Yale University Press, 1963) pp. 27–28, 44.

2. Pedro Ramet, *Nationalism and Federalism in Yugoslavia 1963–1983* (Bloomington, IN: Indiana University Press, 1984) pp. xv–xviii.

3. Pedro Ramet, op. cit., pp. 142–144. Also see Andrew Borowiec, *Yugoslavia After Tito* (New York: Praeger Publications, 1977) pp. 30–44.

4. See the interview of Milosevic in *Le Monde* (July 12, 1989) p. 6.

5. See, for example, Marjan Korosic, *Jugoslovenske Kriza* (Zagreb: Naprijed, 1989).

6. Marlise Simons, "In Slovenia, Link to Rest of Nation Weakens," *New York Times* (February 13, 1990), p. A12.

7. For conceptual assessment of cults, see Daniel N. Nelson, "Charisma, Control and Coercion," *Comparative Politics* (October, 1984), pp. 1–16.

8. Henry Kamm, *New York Times,* (February 2, 1989); also see statement by Petar Simic of the JNA from *Narodna Armija* as translated in FBIS-Eastern Europe 90-021 (January 31, 1990), p. 77.

9. See Buncic's comments as translated in Foreign Broadcast Information Service, East European Report 89-145 (July 31, 1989), pp. 55–56.

10. Of 188,000 personnel in the JNA, 104,000 are conscripts—of whom more than 25% are now ethnic Albanians. Assuming current demographic trends, this proportion will rise to 50% by 2005. See Bozo Kovac, "U potreba oruzja—Zakonita," *Vjesnik* (April 6, 1989).

11. Branko Horvat, *Jugoslavensko Drustvo u Krizi* (Zagreb: Globus, 1986).

12. Business International, *Business East Europe,* Vol. XIX, No. 3 (January 15, 1990), p. 19. Also see *Monthly Bulletin of Statistics,* UN Statistical Office, Vol. XLIV, No. 1 (January, 1990).

13. Ewa Berkowic has done the most thorough empirical study of these phenomena. See her *Socijalne Nejednakosi u Jugoslaviji* (Belgrade: Ekonomik and Ekonomski Institut, 1986); a broad indictment of political inequalities reinforcing economic ones is the volume issued by the Institute of Sociology at the University of Belgrade entitled *Drustvene Nejednakosti* (Beograd: Institut za socioloska istrazivanja Filozofskog Fakulteta u Beogradu, 1987).

14. Marlise Simons, "Yugoslavia on the Brink," *New York Times* (January 24, 1990), p. 1.

15. Judy Dempsey, "Yugoslavia May Act Against More Enterprises," *The Financial Times* (September 15, 1987), p. 3. Also see Henry Kamm, "Financial Scandal Shakes Yugoslav Leaders," *The New York Times* (September 10, 1987), p. 16.

16. Ramet, op. cit., pp. 138–139.

17. Discussion of situation between Albanians and Serbs see "Milosevic Interview on Serbia—Slovenia Dispute," from Pristina *Rilindja* (December 22,

1989) as translated in FBIS-Eastern European 90-3 (January 3, 1990), p. 99. Also see Marlise Simons, "Belgrade Steps up Army's Presence in Kosovo" *The New York Times* (February 8, 1990).

18. "Yugoslavia Military Press for Change," *The Financial Times* (September 25, 1987), p. 2.

19. Dragan Colovic, untitled commentary from the "Sunday at 10" program (October 11, 1987) as translated in FBIS-Eastern Europe 87-197 (October 13, 1987), p. 62.

20. Judy Dempsey, *Financial Times* (February 1, 1989).

21. Aleksander Tijanic, "Promene u armiji," *Nin*, #2022 (October 1, 1989), p. 11.

22. See interview with Vice Admiral Stane Brevet carried over Tanjug Domestic Service on July 5, 1989, as translated by FBIS-Eastern Europe 89-130 (July 10, 1989), p. 56.

23. The Slovene Youth Journal *Mladina* was most vocal in its anti-military rhetoric. Attitudes towards the JNA were generally negative, however. See, for example, Marko Lopusina, "Strategija domina," *Interviju* (April 15, 1988); the military's reaction is exemplified by S. Petrovic, "Military Guards Stoned," *Politika* (June 18, 1988), as translated in FBIS-Eastern Europe 88-170 (June 22, 1988), p. 70.

24. David L. Larson, *United States Foreign Policy Toward Yugoslavia 1943–1963* (Washington, D.C.: University Press of America, 1979), pp. 180–250.

25. *The Military Balance 1989–1990* (London: The International Institute for Strategic Studies, 1989), pp. 92, 249.

26. IMF, *Direction of Trade Statistics*, 1989, p. 418.

3

New Politics and the Army in Bulgaria

If the revolutionary changes of 1989–1990 throughout central, eastern and southeastern Europe are to lead towards competitive democracies and demilitarized societies in a region long known for its rigid authoritarianism, armed forces must "fit" into the new systems. The military institutions of Warsaw Pact states will, necessarily, *join* the popular movement towards democracy by accepting elected civilian authorities and defending them against extremism *or* they will remain uncertain and potentially disruptive political actors. There is no room for a middle course.

The military is not a bystander in the course of far-reaching political change. Precisely how armed forces enter domestic politics, and why their political roles vary, have been subjects of an extensive academic literature.[1]

The Bulgarian People's Army (BPA), and other militaries of Eastern Europe that had been closely intertwined with ruling communist parties, have no choice but to find the basis for a new relationship with political authority—authority that, for the first time in decades, resides largely in the *state*.

In this chapter, I review several principal political changes in Bulgaria during recent years and consider their effects on the armed forces. My concern is both to document the process of systemic change and to identify the BPA's role as an actor in that process.

Propellants of Change

The lowered profile of the Bulgarian Socialist (erstwhile communist) Party (BSP) was confirmed by national elections of June 10—moved up from November in light of the continuing unrest and the Party's political erosion. Although the BSP won 48% of the popular vote in the first round, it no longer has the political field to itself. After action by the

Bulgarian parliament on January 15, 1990, the Bulgarian Communist Party (BCP) lost its constitutionally guaranteed political monopoly, and both the long subservient Agrarian Party as well as opposition groups linked under the Union of Democratic Forces (UDF) banner were formidable opponents in the elections. Within the BCP itself, factions began to compete for control, with pragmatic concerns of power far outweighing ideological views. A name change for the main components of the party—absent were the most Stalinist elements which refused most reforms—was part of the effort to divest themselves of prior regimes' repression and corruption.

Political changes, while slower than elsewhere in communist Europe (Albania being the only exception), are nevertheless fundamental. A new Bulgarian political system, affected by the years of communist rule but very distinct from the past forty-five years, is emerging. External events obviously played a large role in creating the opportunity for democratic voices to be heard in Bulgaria. But Gorbachev's willingness to step away from the Brezhnev Doctrine, and to accept the outcomes of domestic political processes in Eastern Europe, provided a "green light," not the propellant for change.

Domestic pressures for such a transformation accumulated throughout the 1980s, but were particularly forceful in 1989. Events elsewhere in Eastern Europe and the USSR intensified this surge of anti-Zhivkov, anti-BCP sentiment, but there were indigenous factors that created the original impetus for change. Foremost among those domestic conditions were (1) the Turkish national minority issue, (2) the failure of limited economic restructuring, and (3) the intra-party conflicts and electoral competition.

The Turkish Minority Issue

Although a detailed examination of each "propellant" of change in Bulgaria is beyond the scope of this chapter, the role of these principal factors can be sketched. Most volatile, of course, has been the Turkish minority issue and its many facets.

On the surface, the 1980s tensions arose from a clearcut cause: Todor Zhivkov, then Bulgarian Communist Party leader, made a decision in 1984 to inaugurate a campaign to change Turkish-sounding surnames of one million or more Bulgarian citizens to a Bulgarian-sounding equivalent.[2] This campaign was undertaken both through pressure exerted by bureaucrats at birth registration bureaus, but also in public media. Zhivkov's efforts were not directed only at name changes, but also at practices of the Islamic faith such as circumcision and fasting that the government argued were dangers to public health. These actions were viewed by Bulgaria's Islamic minority—both of Turkish and Bulgarian extraction (the latter referred to as Pomaks)—as an attack on their faith and culture, precipitating a rapid escalation of tension in areas heavily inhabited by Moslems. Demonstrations, strikes, and isolated cases of bombings at train stations and other locations during the mid-1980s can be attributed to Zhivkov's insistence that assimilation be effected and that a "single Bulgarian nation" be assured during his regime.

But Zhivkov was not the first Bulgarian leader to make such an argument. Indeed, at the core of the assimilation campaign was the presumption that most Turkish-surnamed individuals were, indeed, Bulgarian whose families in generations past had taken Turkish names as a means of self-protection during Ottoman rule. This was always, however, a weak justification since the political motives were transparent, and the claim that *anyone* in the Balkans is "pure" Bulgarian mixes poorly with a realistic appraisal of the region's history and record-keeping imprecision.[3] Regardless of whether one accepts lower or higher figures for the number of ethnic Turks or followers of Islam in Bulgaria—ranging from 800,000 to 1.4 million—any government effort to deny self-identity and freedom to practice key components of their faith would foster resistance.

Whatever Zhivkov's motivation in 1984, we can be certain that ethnic strife heightened the perception among Bulgarians *and* minority groups that the regime was anachronistic and damaging to the country's well-being. Those who consider themselves Bulgarian by birth and family lineage are not necessarily tolerant of Turkish/Moslem complaints, and there *is* an undeniable animosity towards Turks that may have historical roots dating to five centuries of Ottoman domination. But the vast majority of ethnic Bulgarians seem not to desire policies that will agitate Turks and endanger social peace. Zhivkov's forcible assimilation policy was not, for the most part, supported by Bulgarians. Educated Bulgarians, particularly those who had contacts with the West, understood fully that the Turkish minority issue was damaging the country's international image and had the potential to create economic harm through boycotts and other measures. By 1989, condemnations from international organizations were mounting—most importantly from the Council of Europe's Parliamentary Assembly, the Organization of the Islamic Conference, and the Helsinki Review Conference in Vienna during 1988.[4]

Active opposition from within the Turkish communities was disorganized at first and was entirely unable to mount resistance to the January 1985 repression of protests against the inauguration of the name-changing/ assimilation campaign. But by 1988, three years of ongoing harassment and intimidation had led to the formation of civil rights groups such as the Democratic League for the Defense of Human Rights (founded on November 15, 1988 by just a dozen ethnic Turks who had been imprisoned by the communist regime). These Turkish organizations became loosely tied to other political movements in 1989, all pushing for radical change in Bulgarian politics—e.g., the Discussion Club for the Support of Glasnost and Perestroika, Eco-Glasnost, *Podkrepa* (Support), and ultimately a large umbrella organization, the Union of Democratic Forces (UDF).

Between May 19 and 21, 1989, large demonstrations against Zhivkov's policies took place in Turkish communities in northeastern Bulgaria—one of the two regions of Turkish ethnic concentration—particularly in Razgrad. A couple days later, large and violent protests erupted in towns closer to the Turkish frontier, in southeastern Bulgaria, most notably in Dzhebel, Kurzhali, and Haskovo. Bulgarian security and military forces blockaded roads, used tear gas and truncheons, and employed firearms on a number of occasions. Reports of deaths were confirmed by the Bulgarian news agency, although the official acknowledgement—first of three dead and eventually of eight fatalities[5]—was far lower than other estimates which ranged as high as several dozen.

Over the next several months, at least 310,000 ethnic Turks left Bulgaria. This mass exodus, almost all of whom entered Turkey, was begun when Bulgarian secret police forcibly expelled those accused of being ringleaders of ethnic protests. The flow of people was halted only on August 22, 1989, when Turkey reimposed visa requirements on Bulgarian citizens who wished to enter Turkey.[6] These deportations, numbering in the thousands, precipitated the flight of entire communities who, fearing further reprisals, abandoned their homes and jobs and sought asylum in Turkey. Then–Foreign Minister Mladenov and Prime Minister Atanosov argued that these hundreds of thousands flooding the border were merely tourists seeking to visit relatives; Sofia denied entirely that any coercion had initiated the exodus.

The economic and social consequences of such a huge and sudden departure, and in 1990 the return of some Turks who now want their property and jobs back, have been immense.[7] Because of the birthrate among ethnic Turks—a growth rate in excess of 2.0% per year—Turks constitute a disproportionate part of the work force in the country as a whole, and particularly in the northeast and southeast. Most of those who fled during the spring and summer of 1989 were employed, and the labor force was depleted severely in many areas. In some towns, where the Turkish population was small, only a 5% loss occurred; in other places, however, 40% or more of the work force departed.[8] The regime tried to consider a number of countermeasures, and did try to mobilize a variety of other labor sources including students and some army conscripts. The closing of factories, however, was not avoided, and a variety of agricultural products dropped greatly in output because of the Turks' departure. As will be discussed below, efforts to effect "marketization" in Bulgaria—to move away from central planning and state ownership—have had enough trouble without confronting additional dislocations due to mass population movement.

Perhaps worse than these economic losses, however, were the heightened animosities generated between Turks and Bulgarians within Bulgaria (and, of course, between Sofia and Ankara). Human rights guarantees for Turks, and an end to the assimilation campaign, were sought by several opposition groups, but these were not representative of mass public opinion. In the Bulgarian public writ large, one finds both a recognition that forcing people to change their names was wrong *and* a substantial suspicion of Turkey and Turks in Bulgaria. Even groups such as Eco-Glasnost, which has supported the drive for statutory protection for Turkish religious and cultural rights, evoke a fear that the Turks will ". . . want something else . . ." in the future.[9]

Plans by the post-Zhivkov government to grant additional rights to ethnic minorities—to rescind all of the Zhivkov policies officially, and to create statutory guarantees for linguistic, religious and cultural practices— generated public protest in January 1990. The decision had been made on December 20, but it was not until after the holidays that protests had been organized. Although there were suspicions that hard-line communists were trying to fan the flames of ethnic unrest to discredit the reformist ethos that was sweeping through Bulgaria, the underlying fears of "giving the Turks too much" were real. Coupled with demonstrations in front of the Grand National Assembly were work stoppages throughout the country, some of which continued into February. Demands for the deportation of all Turks, and against provisions for enhanced civil liberties for minorities, were heard frequently during early 1990.[10] This nationalism and intolerance will almost certainly recur.

For the Bulgarian military, the vengeful return of ethnic schisms is highly dangerous. Although further discussion of the armed forces' place in current political dynamics follows, it is important to underscore how susceptible the military is to this kind of domestic unrest. Largely based on conscripts, the Bulgarian armed forces have a draft pool disproportionately composed of ethnic Turks and Pomaks, among whom the birth rate is substantially higher. Thus, instead of constituting 13–15% of draft-age young men, the Turk/Pomak element is about 30% of the conscript pool. Given the roles now being filled by the Army in the northeast and southeast of the country, no important functions (even in the construction and logistics units to which Turks have been traditionally assigned) can be entrusted to such draftees in areas of unrest. Further, of course, access of Turks to weapons and ammunition storage facilities through military service must be carefully monitored, consuming additional manpower from among the "reliable" ethnic Bulgarians.

Economic Issues

Bulgaria's economic problems have also accumulated and contributed to the course of political events. In some respects these economic problems have been directly linked to the Zhivkov-initiated assimilation policy that created such acrimony in the 1980s. Years before the departure of over 300,000 Turks left dangerous labor gaps in many regions, the communist regime had attempted to "bulgarianize" the society and economy. Turks and Pomaks in management positions, particularly in the agricultural sector, were forced to submit to the humiliation of changing surnames or lose their positions. Many refused between 1984 and 1989, and added to the flight from agricultural employment that had already been induced by the communist regime's effort to promote industry and, particularly, high-technology.[11]

A severe agricultural labor shortage—present in large part because of the very low Bulgarian birth rate over the past two decades—has been particularly evident in the early autumn when, during harvesting, students have been brought by the truckloads out to collective farms for picking beets, potatoes and other crops.[12]

Agriculture, of course, was an Achilles' heel of socialist economics for years, and Bulgaria was no exception. Despite over a decade of "reform" prior to Zhivkov's ouster in 1989, Bulgarian agriculture had failed to respond,[13] suffered repeated declines in production that were barely offset by higher output in some years[14] and had diminished in importance for the country's exports.[15]

Bulgaria's economic difficulties, however, are not confined to the agricultural sector. Indeed, the myriad of reform documents, decrees, and pronouncements that emanated from the Zhivkov regime from 1978 through the 1980s were in response to unambiguous signals that the system was collapsing, and that something drastic had to be done. Yet, it become dramatically clear that no one could ensure implementation of reforms without accompanying political changes. The New Economic Mechanism (NEM) that was introduced with great fanfare in 1978 was revised again and again in the 1980s.

By 1985, the failure of Bulgaria's NEM was undeniable, as was the necessity of more thorough and fundamental changes.[16] Perhaps the most important step taken by the Zhivkov regime—encouraged not only by domestic economic problems but also by the Gorbachev leadership in Moscow—was the serious movement towards self-management envisioned by the 1987 New Regulations on Economic Activity.[17] Unfortunately for Bulgaria, this and accompanying legislation in 1987 provided anything but a clear direction. Indeed, commentary about this final stage of Zhivkov's juggling of economic policy implied the poor guidance and uncertain consequences of such new regulations.[18]

Results of the Bulgarian NEM and other reformist initiatives were paltry through 1989. Western assessments of reform programs, and specifically of self-management, the pricing system, and other components of reform, found them to be seriously flawed.[19]

Bulgaria's economic condition by 1990 was, then, not surprising. A rapidly growing level of imports coupled with declining agricultural output and labor shortages meant that Bulgaria did not produce enough, or enough of high quality, to pay for its imports. Foreign debt escalated rapidly, shortages of basic foodstuffs spread, and inflation rose.

For Bulgaria's armed forces, the tightening economic noose has taken a toll on sectors that undergirded the country's very high military effort.[20] Heavy machine building, energy, and construction have all been branches of Bulgarian industry that suffered a decline in output in 1989 vis-à-vis 1988. The electronics industry's output grew, but labor productivity in that branch was relatively stagnant, meaning that much of the increase was capital intensive.[21] If Bulgaria now moves decisively away from state ownership and central planning, then the military will lose its capacity to assure that the branches of industry most critical to a "military economy" receive preferential access to resources. And, were the BPA required to buy at market prices the weapons it has become accustomed to deploying, its commanding officers will be in for a rude awakening.

From both the standpoint of the country's work force and industrial performance, then, economic signals run headlong into what we may presume to be interests of the BPA in a post-communist Bulgaria.

Party and Electoral Dynamics

Finally, of course, currents of change have buffeted the ruling party which, as noted above, changed its name and principal leaders during late 1989 and early 1990. Todor Zhivkov's resignation on November 10, 1989 ended, under duress, a 35-year rule that had been marked by reluctant reformism, and hesitant moderation of the Bulgarian Communist Party's stranglehold on political processes.[22]

Zhivkov did not confront massive civil disobedience as had Honecker and Krenz in East Germany or Milos Jakes in Czechoslovakia. Although there had been an incremental birth of dissident groups in 1988–1989 in Bulgaria,[23] October and early November, 1989 witnessed more visible dissent as pro-democracy rallies of several thousand people were held on a number of occasions. The protests that seemed to have had the most political effect were those of November 3–5 1989, during the meeting of the CSCE environmental conference in Sofia. These gatherings generated many ancillary protests throughout the country, often with the unofficial ecological group "Eco-Glasnost" as an organizer, and garnered substantial international press coverage. The formation of a "Club for the Support of Perestroika and Glasnost," as noted earlier, also occurred in the fall of 1989, and was interwoven in membership and purpose with "Eco-Glasnost." Its first conference was also held in Sofia during the first week of November 1989.

That these relatively small and not very destabilizing events occurred in November did not, in and of themselves, bring about Zhivkov's demise. Certainly, the ethnic tensions and economic crises discussed above formed the deeper roots of Zhivkov's apparently sudden departure.

But we can also be sure that Mikhail Gorbachev played some role—and probably a significant one—in the BCP Politburo's actions. Most noteworthy in all that happened in November was the elevation of Petar Mladenov, for over a decade the Bulgarian foreign minister, to the Party leadership. Mladenov, who was both far younger and probably much more reformist than other Politburo members, was probably not the BCP's "internal" choice, and there is strong circumstantial evidence that Gorbachev may have encouraged the Bulgarian party to leap beyond incremental change to a younger, reformist image.[24]

Within days after Zhivkov's resignation, indications of how significant November 1989 would become in modern Bulgarian history began to be apparent. On November 13, a panel of the Bulgarian Supreme Court heard the Prokurator's office argue that previous efforts to deny legal registration to "Eco-Glasnost" had been wrong, and that the Supreme Court should consider the case on appeal. Legalization of Eco-Glasnost and other organizations soon followed, but this act in November represented a turning point—where the government ceased to oppose each and every expression of independent, critical opinion.[25]

By mid to late December 1989, popular expectations for rapid socio-economic and political transformations once Zhivkov was gone had begun to spill over into widespread public protests. The independent trade union *Podkrepa* quickly became, within a few weeks, an important political force, with its leader Konstantin Trenchev speaking to rallies and issuing ultimatums—that the BCP had to submit to dialogue with opposition groups, or face a nation-wide general strike.[26] Turks and Bulgarian Moslems also surfaced to demand an end to governmental persecution. These

The Army in Bulgaria 63

demonstrations both preceded and followed the BCP's agreement to enter into discussions with opposition groups beginning on January 3, 1990.

The initial round of talks between the BCP and various opposition groups did not, in fact, begin until January 16—following a one-day Parliamentary session that, as noted above, removed from the Bulgarian constitution terminology that had guaranteed the BCP a dominant ("leading") political role. This parliamentary action was a direct response to vocal demands made on January 13-14 by perhaps as many as 50,000 people in central Sofia—demands that included the resignation of the premier (Georgi Antanosov), the scheduling of a two-stage election (first in those districts held by close Zhivkov associates, and a general election in November), an investigation of the secret police ("Department Six") and other issues.

These huge rallies, assembled by the joint action of more than a dozen opposition groups under the UDF banner, made it clear that the Communist Party could no longer avert a fundamental change in its role. Even after parliamentary action to end the BCP's political monopoly, however, the first "Round Table" exchange was conflictual. Initial demands of the opposition had little to do with public policy, and a great deal to do with having access to the basic resources that would enable them to function effectively (office space, equipment to print newsletters, etc.).[27]

In order to participate in these discussions with the government, the various opposition groups had organized themselves into the UDF, the most well-known components of which are *Podkrepa* and Eco-Glasnost. The UDF President at that time, Zhelyu Zhelev, led the opposition delegation. The government's negotiating team was headed by Andrei Lukanov, a member of the BCP Politburo and leader of the Party's parliamentary group.

The rapid pace of events continued on January 18th with the arrest of Todor Zhivkov, indicted by a National Assembly commission for inciting ethnic hostilities and unauthorized use of state property. Less than two weeks later, on January 30, more than 2750 delegates at the Extraordinary 14th BCP Congress (held one year earlier than planned) heard Petar Mladenov offer to form a coalition government until elections would be held—and proposed that these be held in May as opposed to the time preferred by the opposition (November).[28] Prime Minister Antanosov and the cabinet resigned, presumably in order to make this offer more difficult to refuse. Nevertheless, the UDF spokesman, Petar Beron, quickly rejected the Mladenov idea suggesting that it was just a ploy to draw the UDF into the establishment, but did indicate the opposition's agreement to going ahead with a late spring, 1990 election.[29]

The Bulgarian Communist Party congress was nevertheless of great importance. Major structural and personnel changes in the BCP were effected over considerable resistance from conservative delegates. Petar Mladenov was removed from the role of party leader, and replaced by Aleksandar Lilov (whose title is Chairman of the Presidency of the Supreme Party Council), who had clashed with Zhivkov in 1983 over the failure to pursue reforms. Other younger people were brought into a newly formed and smaller (153 members as opposed to 311) "Supreme Party Council" that replaced the Central Committee. The Politburo, also, was renamed a "Presidium" and cut to only four people. Mladenov remained as interim President of Bulgaria, and Andrei Lukanov was soon thereafter tapped to form a new all-communist government as prime minister.[30] Ironically, this was the first all-communist government in the post World War II period, since the BCP's long-time sycophant, the Agrarian National Union, ended its subservience. A name change was also discussed at the Congress, but was highly controversial. In late March, an intra-Party referendum was held, and a change to the "Bulgarian Socialist Party" was approved—but far from unanimously. Indeed, Radio Sofia reported that of the Party's membership, 20% did not vote, and 14% of those who *did* vote cast a negative ballot.[31]

The BSP thus entered the electoral fray with a new set of leaders (Mladenov, Lilov, Lukanov), a new name, structure and commitment to reforms, positioning itself as a "renewed" force ". . . a bit further left than center."[32]

The electoral campaign was primarily a contest between the BSP and the UDF, although a variety of historical, former follower and new parties also competed beside the UDF. Roughly sixty parties and movements were "registered" to campaign, of which thirteen were linked under the UDF banner.[33] An international team of observers for the Bulgarian electoral campaign issued a report which indicated a positive "overall assessment" of ". . . prospects for free, fair and meaningful elections. . . ." There was praise from this election monitoring group for the implementation of procedures to ensure a proper vote. Nevertheless, there were concerns expressed about ". . . the inequity of resources available to the competing parties . . ." and some reports of ". . . harassment of citizens and potential voters by local officials. . . ."[34] These complaints, of course, were voiced repeatedly by the UDF and other opposition parties.[35]

Tallies of voting on June 10 indicated a strong showing by the BSP, with slightly more than 48% of the total, and the UDF-affiliated candidates receiving around 32%.[36] The opposition won Sofia, but lost badly in most smaller cities and the countryside. This translated, after the June 17 runoff, into about an even split among the 400 seats in the Grand National Assembly between the BSP and all other parties. The formation of a BSP-dominated cabinet was thus assured, although some halting efforts at coalition-building were between the BSP and minor parties. Stunned by their defeat, and angry at what they perceive to be manipulation of media by the BSP, the opposition mounted large protests (reaching 100,000 people on June 12) in Sofia denouncing the election results and demanding more democracy. Throughout the summer tension mounted until, in late August, rioting led to the burning of BSP headquarters in Sofia, and near anarchy.

The Bulgarian People's Army was by no means insulated from the spring 1990 political campaign and subsequent turmoil. Indeed, the armed forces became both an issue with respect to voting procedures and an issue of debate among the parties. The same international election monitors who commended Bulgarian efforts to establish fair electoral procedures expressed concern ". . . about the prospects for equitable campaign opportunities among military personnel." Soldiers as independent voters are certainly a new thought within Bulgaria, and there was doubt about the access of all parties and candidates to the voters in the army, as well as the degree to which soldiers would actually feel "free" to vote their choice. The latter concern arose since initial plans were to have troops vote "on base" or in adjacent military clubs, both options being seen by the opposition as limiting the free choice of voters in the armed forces.[37]

The Bulgarian Electoral Commission articulated standards for political activity among members of the armed forces, and sought to respond to concerns of foreign and domestic critics of the electoral process.[38] Campaigning by members of the regular armed forces *or* militia, however, became an item for debate prior to the election, and the BSP was quick to pick up on cases in which the UDF was publicly supported by officers, thus violating the Electoral Commission's rules.[39]

More important, the Army became involved in debates about defense issues in the platforms of parties which competed in the June 10 parliamentary elections. Although little of the BPA's internal discussion about the parties and politicians was made public, some of the commentary by the military was published.

Perhaps most revealing was the *Narodna Armiya* article on May 14, 1990 by the Deputy Minister of National Defense, General Yordan Mutafchiev. In this essay, Mutafchiev argues that a ". . . struggle between rational and emotional arguments is [being] conducted not only in the squares, preelection rallies, meetings, and the mass media. It also emerges . . . in the basic preelection documents adopted by the parties . . . where sober analysis and reasonable ideas are mixed with agitation, promises and wishes."[40]

Mutafchiev implies that certain "realities" must be considered by the political parties and electoral coalitions—that is, a threatening security environment for Bulgaria originating from Turkish armed forces, the continued existence of NATO, and the American bases to the south. Further, while accepting the notion of smaller armed forces, the deputy defense minister notes critically that the UDF platform did not speak of defense reliability and efficiency, while the BSP and the National Agrarian Union were credited with being ". . . more satisfactory. . . ."[41] Clearly, the UDF is seen as crossing a line unacceptable to the Bulgarian Army, and as advocating a defense policy incompatible with reliable and sufficient forces.

In significant respects, then, the Bulgarian military was drawn into the competitive political arena. Its senior officers have tried to defend what they see as its interests, to make clear the policy preferences of the High Command, and to deflect criticism about electoral procedures among military personnel. Forced to move out from beneath the wing of a single ruling party, the army has begun a halting and somewhat awkward participation in political contests, seeking to ensure that whoever governs from *state* positions knows the military's interests and does not act against them. Simultaneously, the military watched with alarm the growing inability of state authorities to constrain political turmoil.

The Army and Bulgaria's Transitions

How has the Bulgarian People's Army (BPA)—the armed forces of Bulgaria—contributed to, or been affected by the social and political movements within the country? How will it (the BPA) respond, and what are likely roles for the Army in Bulgaria's political future? From a distance, there appeared to be a close symbiotic relationship between the Bulgarian Communist Party (BPA) of Todor Zhivkov's regime and the Army.[42] Such appearances would lead us to presume that the BPA was not anxious to see this link disrupted by fundamental political change.

The Army's tie to the BCP, however, was never primarily one of ideological affinity or, indeed, of political orientation at all. There is ample evidence to the contrary, with both empirical findings and inferential assessments pointing towards a military with dubious loyalties to communist rule.[43]

Bulgaria's military officers were loyal less to Zhivkov and the BCP than to the army as an institution, and the military's access to resources. As long as the pipeline for manpower and material resources was wide open, with the country maintaining the highest per capita level of armed forces in the Warsaw Pact outside the USSR while devoting huge proportions of its central budget to military expenditures, the BPA was a potential Zhivkov ally. But the resource base began to be endangered by the simultaneous disruption of social equilibrium, brought on by Zhivkov's ethnic assimilation policy, and the dangerous economic trends that Zhivkov's fumbling economic policy could not reverse. Judgments about such dangers to the military brought about ever-growing support for removing Zhivkov.

The personification of the army's interests has been General Dobri Dzhurov who, for twenty-eight years, was Bulgaria's defense minister. Even at seventy-five years old, Dzhurov certainly held the key to power during the critical months from late 1989 to mid-1990. After legitimating elections, some of his ability to affect immediate political processes waned—*but* there is little doubt that his continuity and visibility from November 1989 to August 1990 were not accidental. Whereas then-President Petar Mladenov, Party Leader Aleksadr Lilov and Premier Andrei Lukanov gained an electoral victory on which to base the Bulgarian Socialist Party's "right to rule," Dzhurov has been someone with authority quite apart from the political fray.

Precisely how it was that Todor Zhivkov stepped down on November 10, 1989 may never be fully unraveled. Some small demonstrations had occurred, and underlying economic and ethnic tensions were clear and present dangers to the regime. Two unintended "allies" in the removal of Zhivkov, however, could have been Gorbachev and Dzhurov. Without any communications or contact, the Soviet leadership and Bulgarian military command had come to the same conclusion—Zhivkov's time had run out, and that the Party stood a far better chance of surviving a political transformation if it stepped out "in front of the curve." To do so required, first, sacking Zhivkov. The BCP Politburo would have never taken that step, however, without Soviet insistence and Dzhurov's assurance that the Army would neither defend Zhivkov nor take action of its own. Only Dzhurov could have been asked for such a guarantee, and only he could have provided it.

Petar Mladenov as foreign minister under Zhivkov and Dobri Dzhurov as defense minister had served together in the Council of Ministers since the early 1970s. Although little is known about their association with one another, it is plausible that Dzhurov viewed Mladenov as the least objectionable alternative to become party leader among the small list of reform-oriented BCP figures. At the very least, Mladenov was a "known quantity." We do not know if a deal was struck involving Dzhurov and BCP leaders. Associates of Dzhurov were, however, moved into key positions within the government, and the defense minister himself remained a locus of power that was impossible for the government to ignore.

Principal among those initial appointments was that of Colonel General Atanas Semerdzhiev to become minister of internal affairs. Six weeks

68

after the ouster of Zhivkov, Georgi Tanev was removed as minister. Tanev, perhaps more than any other person in Zhivkov's inner circle, had been identified with the assimilation campaign against Turks and other minorities as well as activities of the "Sixth Department"—spying and intimidation within Bulgaria against the country's own citizens.

Semerdzhiev (who turned 66 in 1990) shares much of Dzhurov's background including service, in World War II, as a party member in the "Chavdar" Partisans.[44] He then served in the BPA officer corps, rising in rank—performing well in command roles and completing mandatory education in Soviet academies. By the time he was 40, Semerdzhiev had been tapped by Dzhurov to become chief of the general staff and then Dzhurov's deputy minister of defense. Like his superior, Semerdzhiev remained in these posts for well over two decades.[45] One must assume that Semerdzhiev has much to owe Dzhurov for his career and prominence.

But Semerdzhiev was forced to resign from the Ministry of Internal Affairs in late July because of the same issues tainting Mladenov. Semerdzhiev was not, however, denied prominence, becoming vice-president, now serving "under" the UDF president, Zhelev. General Stoyan Stoyanav, also a Dzhurov associate, replaced Semerdzhiev—and lasted only a month, until arsonists destroyed BSP headquarters, and police inaction received heavy criticism from the new president—Zhelev—and Prime Minister Lukanov. An interior minister acceptable to the army seems still necessary, but the new minister may now be required to exhibit greater responsiveness to civilian authority.

After Mladenov's resignation, and changes in the Ministry of Internal Affairs, Dzhurov's position as Defense Minister became a holdover from the prior regime that seemed anachronistic. In late September 1990, Lukanov (urged by UDF President Zhelev) appointed Deputy Defense Minister Mutafchiev as the new Defense Minister. But Mutafchiev had been Dzhurov's hand-picked deputy as well, and this change does not imply a significant assertion of civil authority over the High Command.

Perhaps more indicative of Dzhurov's importance to the government throughout this period had been his visibility from late 1989 through 1990. There has been little effort spared to convey to General Dzhurov that he is appreciated, honored, and needed.[46] Indeed, there may have been too much of such effort. In January, Dzhurov was seen to be more popular than most of the other prominent politicians; by the end of May, however, Lukanov, Mladenov, Lilov, Zhelev (then UDF President), and even Social Democratic Chairman Dertliev received the highest approval rating from larger proportions of the Bulgarian population. Dzhurov's 15% was, however, higher than Podkrepa President Konstantin Trenchev.[47]

The Army in Bulgaria 69

Dzhurov's apparent importance for BSP personages Mladenov, Lilov and Lukanov and for UDF leader Zhelev who became president when Mladenov resigned, enabled the army to spell out its views on policy issues, and to advocate those positions forcefully. Commanders of the Bulgarian armed forces are most concerned about criticisms of the military from various political parties and social groups, and the effect of such an atmosphere on discipline within the army and on the difficulties it may then confront in fulfilling any domestic role. A broader, but related issue is defensive sufficiency—i.e., what are the minimum force and preparedness levels required to fulfill basic tasks of the Bulgarian armed forces?

On these matters, the Army's voice has been unequivocal. *Narodna Armiya* carried a number of articles in the months leading up to the June 10 election in which the armed forces were portrayed as unfairly maligned by supporters of the UDF. Nikolai Tsvetkov, identified as a captain in the Bulgarian Army, was the author of an article in early May 1990 that told of a young NCO who was severely beaten by UDF youths in Sofia. Tsvetkov then goes on to question why the opposition has not condemned such actions. In the same issue, Captain Ivan Genov alleges that there is an effort to ". . . draw the army into political passions and election struggles . . ." and thereby to ". . . test the army's role in providing stability to society. . . ."[48] Genov argues that the army has no intention other than to "cast ballots like all other Bulgarians."[49]

The UDF was also criticized for having advocated a so-called "small but strong army" and a one-year army training period. Colonel General Vasil Zikulov, writing in *Narodna Armiya* in late May, characterizes these elements of the opposition's defense platform as steps that would ". . . jeopardize our national security." A one-year training period, according to Zikulov, would mean that only 50% of the soldiers in the army would be sufficiently trained for combat at any one time, while suggestions of only six month active duty are rejected entirely. Zikulov explicitly compares the Bulgarian forces with those of Turkey, and insists that "we should by no means allow our troop's training to be inferior to that of the Turkish Army."[50] Zikulov returns, however, to what must be most bothersome to all career officers about the new politics of Bulgaria—i.e., how easily it is in an election campaign to ". . . inspire a negative attitude toward the military service, [and] to incite soldiers against officers. . . ." Zikulov continues:

. . . this leads to a weakening of discipline, it undermines combat readiness, and affects our motherland's security in the long run. *No serious political party that claims the right of ruling Bulgaria in the near future should ever admit such a careless attitude in discussing the questions related to our country's defense.*[51]

Less than two weeks later, another major statement by a military leader was carried in *Otechestven Front* in Sofia. In an extensive interview with this publication, Defense Ministry Spokesman Lieutenant General Radnyu Minchev once again attacked the UDF and the National Agrarian Union for their endorsement of a reduced term for conscription. Minchev's argument against a "professional" army is based on the cost of such a force (that is, recruits would have to be paid much more) and on the idea that a small country such as Bulgaria cannot rely on volunteers to fill out the ranks. Further he rejects alternative service for conscientious objectors, dismisses the idea of assigning conscripts to their home districts, and minimizes the problem of violence against younger recruits by older ones.[52] In short, Minchev gave no ground, resolutely opposed opposition views of military policy, and rejected criticisms of the Army's role in political processes.

That the Bulgarian Army sees its own internal discipline, place in society and access to manpower and material resources *all* endangered by today's politics is very clear. To presume that the military is of one mind, of course, would be misleading. The UDF was able, during the course of the electoral campaign, to attract a number of younger officers to support its candidates.[53]

The officer corps, however, is generally ill-at-ease with trends and prospects. Although endorsing steps such as lower force levels and conversion of defense industry,[54] fears that opposition politicians would denude the military of what commanders see as minimum force and equipment requirements mounted as the campaign continued.

That the BSP gained a plurality on June 10 no doubt relieved the army commanders of their worst nightmares. That turmoil has continued, and that the UDF now controls the presidency, however, requires significant political adjustments. Further, the issues of distance from society, pressure to reduce consumption of resources, and underlying socioeconomic tensions will be quite discomfiting to armed forces accustomed to much more. With Dobri Dzhurov's own appointee as his replacement, the army can be sure that its voice and needs will be heard. But it can no longer be sure that its voice will be the loudest.

Notes

1. Examples of these literatures are plentiful. Certainly the most influential among studies of the politics of the Soviet military have been Roman Kolkowicz, *The Soviet Military and the Communist Party* (Princeton: Princeton University

The Army in Bulgaria

Press, 1967), William E. Odom's article, "The Party-Military Connection: A Critique," in Dale Herspring, ed. *Civil-Military Relations in Communist Systems* (Boulder: Westview, 1978), and Timothy Colton's *Commissars, Commanders, and Civilian Authority: The Structure of Soviet Military Politics* (Cambridge: Harvard University Press, 1979). Examinations of armed forces and society and/or the military in politics within the West or Third World have been undertaken by Morris Janowitz, Samuel Huntington, Gavin Kennedy, and S.E. Finer—just to name a few of the most widely cited. See Morris Janowitz, *The Military in the Political Development of New Nations* (Chicago: University of Chicago Press, 1964), Samuel F. Huntington, *The Soldier and the State* (Cambridge: Harvard University Press, 1959), Gavin Kennedy, *The Military in the Third World* (New York: Charles Scribner's Sons, 1974), and S.E. Finer, *The Man on Horseback, 2nd Edition* (Boulder: Westview, 1988).

2. The outset of this policy was described by Paul Legg, "A Turkish Population Vanishes in Bulgaria," *The Wall Street Journal-Europe* (May 29, 1985).

3. A discussion of both the Ottoman background and data issues is contained in Wolf Oschlies, "Bulgariens Bevolkerung Mitte der 80er Jahre," *Berichte. des Bundesinstituts fur ostwissenschaftliche und internationale Studien* Number 17 (Koln: Bundesintitut, 1986).

4. A few examples of Western commentary on the situation by spring 1989 reveal the level of image damage that Bulgaria had incurred due to Zhivkov's forced assimilation policy. See, for example, William Echikson, "Bulgaria Pays Little Heed to Glasnost When it Comes to Minorities," *Christian Science Monitor* (June 19, 1989), Sam Cohen's "Bulgaria Expels Ethnic Turks: Ankara Seeks Western Help in Crisis," *Christian Science Monitor* (June 8, 1989) and Stephen Asley,"Special Report: Bulgaria and the Ethnic Turks," in Radio Free Europe/ Radio Liberty, *Soviet/East European Report* (July 5, 1989).

5. The Bulgarian News Agency (BTA) dispatch of May 23, 1989 confirmed three deaths. Later, they admitted to eight deaths. See Andrew Mango, "Turkish Exodus From Bulgaria," *The World Today* Vol. 45, Number 10 (October, 1989), p. 166.

6. Mango, "Turkish Exodus From Bulgaria," Ibid.

7. A good overview of the range of socioeconomic problems created by the 1989 exodus is Rada Nikolaev, "Counting the Costs of The Turkish Exodus: The Shortage of Labor" and the same author's "The Social and Economic Problems Caused by the Exodus," both in Radio Free Europe Research, *Bulgarian Situation Report,* Number 9 (October 5, 1989), in Radio Free Europe Research, Vol. 14, No. 40 (October 6, 1989).

8. Discussions of these labor consequences appeared in the Party daily, then named *Rabotnichesko Delo* frequently from June through late 1989. See, for example, the statements of Stoyan Ovcharov to a Parliamentary committee in mid-July in which projections of dramatic labor shortages in some cities were discussed. *Rabotnichesko Delo* (September 4, 1989).

9. An Eco-Glasnost representative in Kurdzhali, as quoted by Glenn Frankel, "Bulgaria Gripped by Fears Amid Steps to Ease Ethnic Conflict," *The Washington Post* (January 14, 1990).

10. See the Associated Press dispatch carried under the title "Slavic Nationalists Continue Protests in Bulgaria," in *Washington Post* (January 7, 1990).

11. A commentary on these intentions was "Bulgaria's Ambitious High-Tech Goals" in *The New York Times* (July 4, 1985), p. 33.

12. A report on the use of students for such agricultural labor was carried in *Narodna Mladezh* (June 14, 1989).

13. Regarding one set of plans for agricultural reform that were never fully implemented, consult the BBC's Summary of World Broadcasts (December 30, 1986).

14. Deborah A. Lamb, "Bulgaria: Performance and Prospects in Trade with the United States and the West" in Joint Economic Committee, U.S. Congress, *East-West Trade: The Prospects to 1985* (Washington, D.C.: U.S. Government Printing Office, 1982), pp. 28–29.

15. Food and live animal imports from the Federal Republic of Germany, for example, more than tripled between 1987 and 1988, while total trade was about the same—i.e., imports of other products (manufactured goods, chemicals, etc.) were reduced in order to obtain necessary food. See the PlanEcon data cited by Marvin R. Jackson, "A Crucial Phase in Bulgarian Economic Reforms," *Berichte des Bundesinstituts fur ostwissenschaftliche und internationale Studien,* Number 72 (Koln: Bundesinstitut, 1989), p. 5.

16. See, for instance, the critical observations made in "Bulgaria Beset by Economic Woes," *Washington Post* (November 8, 1985), p. A33; also "Bulgaria Promises Changes in Economy," *Washington Post* (April 3, 1986), p. A23.

17. *Pravilnik za stopanskata deinost,* in *Durzhaven Vestnik* 3 (1987); discussion of the new economic regulations at the March, 1987 National Party conference was reported in *Rabotnichesko Delo* (March 6, 1987).

18. See, for instance, "As Clear as Yoghurt: Bulgaria's Odd Reform," *The Economist* (August 1, 1987), p. 45; "A Long Wait for Things to Get Better," *New York Times* (October 2, 1987), p. 6; and "All Clear? Economic Reform in Bulgaria," *The Economist* (February 6, 1988), p. 46.

19. Thomas Brey, "Bulgarien zwischen Tradition und Perestrojka: Eine Skizze politischer und wirtschaftlicher Reformansatze," *Osteuropa* 39, 2/3 (February/March, 1989), pp. 260–268, especially 262–265. See also the very thorough examination by Richard J. Crampton, " 'Stumbling and Dusting Off,' or an Attempt to Pick a Path Through the Thicket of Bulgaria's New Economic Mechanism," *East European Politics and Societies* Vol. II, No. 2 (Spring, 1988). Another excellent analysis is Marvin R. Jackson's, "A Crucial Phase in Bulgarian Economic Reforms," op. cit.

20. Concerning Bulgaria's military effort relative to other members of the Warsaw Pact, both in terms of extractive and performance measures, see Daniel N. Nelson, *Alliance Behavior in the Warsaw Pact* (Boulder: Westview, 1986) and Daniel N. Nelson, "Distribution of Military Effort in the Warsaw Pact," in U.S. Congress, Joint Economic Committee, *Pressures for Reform in East Economies* (Washington, D.C.: GPO, 1989).

21. These data were published in *Rabotnichesko delo* (July 22, 1989).

22. Some of the Western reporting on Bulgaria during the late 1980s suggests the Zhivkov-inspired reticence about change. See, for example, "Zhivkov ousts

The Army in Bulgaria 73

backer of Bulgarian Changes," *New York Times* (July 23, 1988), "Why Reform Moves Slowly in Bulgaria," *The Christian Science Monitor* (February 3, 1988), and "Soviet-Style Changes Confuse Bulgarians," *Washington Post* (January 30, 1988).

23. For example, note the report (no by-line) in *The Christian Science Monitor* (January 18, 1989) on "Dissent Rises in Hard-Line Bulgaria."

24. Blaine Harden reported on some of this speculation in "Strong Soviet Influence Suspected in Sudden Departure of Bulgarian Leader," *Washington Post* (November 12, 1989).

25. See Clyde Haberman, "Hearing Cheers Bulgaria's Dissidents," *New York Times* (November 14, 1989).

26. This demand by Trenchev was reported by, among others, a Reuters dispatch of December 27, 1989.

27. Celestine Bohlen, "Opposition's Talks With Communists in Sofia Off to a Rough Start," *The New York Times* (January 17, 1990).

28. Reported in a Reuters dispatch from Sofia of January 30, 1990.

29. See the Associated Press account, printed in *The New York Times* (February 1, 1990), "Bulgaria Opposition Rebuffs Communists on Sharing Power."

30. *Rabotnichesko Delo* (January 30 through February 5) covered the congress thoroughly and in an almost verbatim style, with lengthy excerpts from speeches and debates. Typical of Western press accounts were Marlise Simons, "Bulgarian Leader is Out of Communist Party Job After Stormy Congress," *The New York Times* (February 3, 1990) and Jonathan C. Randal, "Bulgarian Communists Pick Reformist Leader," *Washington Post* (February 3, 1990).

31. As cited by Rada Nikolaev, "The Bulgarian Communist Party After its 'Congress of Renewal,'" in Radio Free Europe Research, *Report on Eastern Europe* (April 4, 1990), p. 6.

32. Interview with Aleksandar Lilov in *Der Spiegel* (March 5, 1990).

33. For an overview as of late March, 1990, see Mihaly Fulop and Laszlo Poti, "An East European Party Census," No. 2 in the *Policy Paper Series* of the Hungarian Institute of International Affairs (Budapest: Hungarian Institute of International Affairs, 1990); see, especially, pp. 8–9.

34. National Democratic Institute for International Affairs, "Bulgaria Pre-Election Survey Report" (Washington, D.C.: May 13–17, 1990), pp. 4, 5.

35. Judy Dempsey, "Bulgarian Opposition Hits Out at Intimidation," *Financial Times* (June 4, 1990).

36. Celestine Bohlen, "Ex-Communists Decisively Lead Bulgaria Voting," *The New York Times* (June 11, 1990).

37. National Democratic Institute, "Bulgaria Pre-Election Survey Report," op. cit., p. 5.

38. Interview with Ivan Efremov, Deputy Chairman of the Central Electoral Commission, in *Narodna Armiya* (May 11, 1990), p. 2.

39. Plamen Enchev. "A Militia Major Is Campaigning for UDF on RFE," *Duma* (May 9, 1990).

40. Lt. General Yordan Mutafchiev, "Issues of Defense in Pre-election Platforms," *Narodna Armiya* (May 14, 1990), pp. 1–4.

41. Ibid.

42. See Daniel N. Nelson, "WTO Mobilization Potential: A Bulgarian Case Study," *Defense Analysis* Vol. 5, No. 1 (1989), pp. 31–44.

43. I have reviewed much of this evidence in my chapter on Bulgaria in Jeffrey Simon, editor, *Force Mobilization: NATO and the Warsaw Pact* (Washington, D.C.: National Defense University Press, 1988), pp. 468–469.

44. Veterans of this Partisan formation have been a dominant element in Bulgarian politics for decades, fighting off a 1965 coup attempt by people who had been officers of a rival "Vratza" Partisan group in World War II.

45. These biographical details are drawn from Djell Engelbrekt, "Shakeup in the Ministry of Internal Affairs," in Radio Free Europe, *Report on Eastern Europe* Vol. 1, Number 20 (May 18, 1990), p. 6.

46. Rada Nikolaev, "The Bulgarian Communist Party After its 'Congress Renewal,' " op. cit., p. 8.

47. BTA dispatch, "Only 30 Percent Believe in Fair Elections" (May 31, 1990) reporting on a survey of 2,760 respondents conducted by the Bulgarian Television Audience Research Unit, as cited by FBIS, Eastern Europe No. 90–106 (June 1, 1990), p. 6.

48. See *Narodna Armiya* (May 9, 1990), pp. 1–3.

49. Ibid.

50. *Narodna Armiya* (May 17, 1990), pp. 1–2.

51. Ibid., emphases added.

52. *Otechestven Front* (May 31, 1990), p. 2.

53. *Duma* (May 9, 1990), p. 2 carried a report, cited earlier (footnote 39) concerning the controversy raised when a militia major compaigned for the UDF and his appeal was carried over RFE.

54. See, for example, the comments of General Khristo Dobrev, Bulgarian Chief of Staff, at the January, 1990 CSCE-sponsored meeting of NATO and WTO military leaders in Vienna reported by R. Jeffrey Smith, "East, West Open Talks on Defense," *Washington Post* (January 17, 1990), p. 15.

4

No Longer Tyranny, Not Yet Democracy: Romania's Perilous Path After Ceausescu

Background

In December 1989, the West applauded both the courage of Romanian citizens as they fought to end the Ceausescu dictatorship and the sensibility of the country's army for joining the battle against Ceausescu's Securitate. First to step into the power vacuum was a shadowy group of erstwhile establishment figures—the National Salvation Front (*Frontul Salvarii Nationale* or FSN)—who had been pushed into exile or political oblivion by Ceausescu because of their criticism of his policies. From the beginning, assessments of who these people were and what motivated their actions varied considerably.[1] Some of those individuals had been in personal contact with each other; however, they had prepared no plan, and had no agenda. For years they had communicated surreptitiously, always sure that the Securitate were watching and listening.[2]

The FSN, with branches it sought to quickly establish throughout the country, established an interim government, named people to ministerial posts and went ahead with military tribunals for Ceausescu's close associates (Emil Bobu, Tudor Postelnicu, Ion Dinca and others who served in the Party's Political Executive Committee) and family (two sons, a daughter and a brother). Ceausescu and his wife, Elena, had been executed on December 25, 1989, after a hasty decision by a few military and FSN people. Ion Iliescu, acting as interim president, together with Petre Roman (prime minister), Sergiu Chelac (then foreign minister) and a few others, formed a core decision-making group that issued edicts.[3] This 11-man executive council, however, spoke for over a hundred people—the "Front"—and had an ill-defined role.

In fact, nothing was well-defined. As one can readily understand, the Front's leaders had no clear cut plan for assuming and maintaining power.

"Government" was, by and large, a function of who protested most loudly, with Iliescu (and others who later resigned from the executive council) promising things to surging crowds in what appears to have been moments of panic. The Front's headquarters was besieged by throngs who backed opposition parties, and it still must be protected by a phalanx of soldiers. Heightening the Front's sense of its own fragile hold on power were mid-February protests by both young army officers and by crowds of angry citizens. At one point, the vice-premier, Gelu Voican-Voiculescu, was physically attacked and rescued only when army units intervened.[4]

Plans for free elections were endangered and the legitimacy of any government to emerge from those elections was threatened by an imposing list of difficulties. The lack of experience with anything like a competitive democracy was, from the moment Ceausescu was deposed, a debilitating condition. Neither the guiding principles nor the specific procedures of such a system are widely understood in Romania, and there was no time to engage in a massive re-education effort. Far more than Poles or Hungarians, Romanians lived in a truly totalitarian state for decades. No one in Romania other than people over sixty-five can recall legitimate public debate or *legal* demonstrations not mobilized by a ruling party.

Related to the absence of democratic learning in Romania is the nature of opposition political parties that declared themselves as participants in the electoral campaign. Several "historical" parties with direct lineage from pre-war parties were reborn, and a number of elderly emigres returned to Bucharest to play leading roles in these organizations. Most prominent among these organizations in spring 1990 were the two largest parties of the 1918–early 1930s period (which also played roles in the 1944–1947 coalition government), the National Liberals and the National Peasants.[5]

The National Liberals, evoking pre-war nationalist sentiments mixed with a vehement commitment to the "free market," were led in the election by Sorin Botez and Radu Campeanu. Botez, now elderly, was a post–World War II Liberal who was sentenced at that time to twenty years of hard labor for his anti-communist politics. Campeanu tried, but failed, to form an electoral alliance between the Liberals and other principal opposition parties, and was himself a candidate for president. In the inter-war period, the Liberals were the political expression of Romania's business elite—a tiny, but very powerful stratum.[6]

Seventy-four year old Cornel Coposu reactivated the National Peasant's Party. Coposu had been the party's leader immediately after the war, and resumed that role more than forty years later. Ion Ratiu, who had departed from Romania more than four decades earlier and had amassed a fortune in Britain, returned to run for President under the National

Peasants banner. Although the National Peasants found younger people to fill many of their other posts, this reemergence of the party was dominated by elderly leaders from another era. Although harboring some monarchist sentiments, the National Peasants were the party of landowners and they retained their advocacy of less government, and regional and local autonomy.

A Social Democratic Party led by Sergiu Cunescu (as executive president) and Dr. Adrian Dimitriu (as honorary chairman, representing the older postwar generation) also re-emerged, seeking links to Romania's industrial workers. The difficulty in making such an appeal became apparent in the elections, and the party fared very poorly. Between the wars, socialists, not communists, held the loyalty of Romania's small industrial working class, and an effort to recreate such an appeal within today's huge stratum of labor may be a key test for Romania's political future.

Among the dozens of other political associations, only four groupings had a chance of electoral viability. Although these proclaimed themselves as parties, each formed around a distinct issue or segment of the population—i.e., intellectuals, environmentalists, students, and ethnic Hungarians. The Front, competing as a party, commanded the loyalty of most urban workers; miners and employees of the huge "23 August" enterprise in Bucharest were, for example, foremost among pro-Front demonstrators in early 1990—a loyalty and reliability not lost on Ion Iliescu and those around him.

There was never any doubt that few of the many competitors had any chance whatsoever of playing a visible role in Romanian politics. The Front was certain to gain a sizeable proportion of the vote due to its immediate linkage to events in December, Iliescu's name recognition, and the organizational head-start it had vis-à-vis opposition parties. But the Liberals and Peasants were thought to have a chance as well, with a coalition government not improbable. Divided as they were, however, the opposition parties were unable to expand their base of support very broadly.

Arguments and accusations concerning intimidation, violence, and character defamation were present almost from the outset of renewed multi-party political activity in January. From a variety of reports, there can be little doubt of efforts to disrupt the campaign and to derail the transition to a competitive system. By whom and against whom was this disruptive effort mounted? Many of the victims of threatening letters or calls, of beatings, theft and vandalism were people running against the FSN; although there were instances of Front candidates being abused, the proportion was far smaller. Yet, both statements by and observation of the Front leaders suggests strongly that they (Iliescu, Roman and their immediate advisors) had neither requested nor did they direct intimidation of their opposition. Instead, there was ample concern in the FSN leadership that they did not control and could not find out who was responsible—and the *militia* (the regular police) in outlying *judete* offered little in the way of assistance, preferring to stay out of the fray.

But various observers did not see it from the Front's perspective. Indeed, there were a number of assessments pointing an accusatory finger at the Front for, at the very least, not condemning the attacks/intimidation on Peasant, Liberal or other parties' candidates.[7] Other claims referred to constraints on the distribution of campaign literature and access to media as well as other procedural irregularities.[8] Liberal and Peasant parties, particularly, tried to raise their complaints as loudly as possible, both through their own press and through foreign media covering the election.[9]

Although the issue of campaign irregularities remained highly contentious, and continued to fuel anti-Iliescu sentiment even after May 20, other important currents emerged during the campaign that will affect Romania's political future.

Most important among these movements generated after Ceausescu was deposed were those with an ethno-nationalist or ecological orientation. In the May elections, both Hungarian identity among the perhaps two million Magyars in Romania and ecology among urban residents emerged as political factors that no government can afford to ignore. Although votes for the Hungarian Democratic Union and Ecologists in National Assembly elections were, together, less than 10% of the total, their support rivaled and/or exceeded that given to "historical" parties. The Front, or succeeding governments, will not be able to govern effectively without acknowledging "green," populist or ethno-nationalist interests embedded in many new parties. Further, of course, these issues will remain indefinitely as volatile concerns that can be used by many factions to disrupt political quiescence.

Of Romania's ethnic divisions, there are many indications that festering antagonisms between Hungarians and Romanians in Transylvania (and between other minorities and the Romanian majority) will infect the country's political future. In the months prior to May 20, a number of incidents were rumored to have occurred involving violence by one ethnic group against another.

Most widely reported in the West were the two days of violence in Tirgu Mures during late March 1990. A number of deaths were reported in these Hungarian-Romanian clashes in the city's downtown district. The origins of this confrontation are cloudy, and there are suspicions that any number of political interests (or the Securitate) may have sought to foment ethnic violence in order to disrupt elections. A new ultra-nationalist group—"Vatra Romaneasca," is primary among those organizations accused by opposition parties of having instigated this incident.[10] In this case, the Romanian Army responded by sending in tanks and armored personnel carriers to separate the two sides, and managed to restore order. Yet, the ethnic schisms are real, and available for exploitation. Hungarian commentary about Tirgu Mures and nationality relations generally featured calls for Hungarians to boycott elections.[11]

Substantial gaps in Romania's socioeconomic infrastructure also plagued the electoral process. Autonomous organizations, from trade unions to professional associations, had no underground existence during the Ceausescu years. The notion that mass organizations operate as adjuncts to a ruling party will not be easily broken in Romania; the Front and other parties continued the practice of mobilizing people for supportive demonstrations, with the Front relying heavily on industrial labor. That Iliescu did not break from this Ceausescu-like tactic was not lost on the Front's many detractors.

Although the Romanian population is highly literate, media remain very underdeveloped in Romania. The Ceausescu regime cut back on television transmissions, and made newspapers and journals unappealing because of their crude propaganda and glorification of Romania's *Conducator.* Nevertheless, taking over and controlling the studios of Romanian Radio and Television was a key part of the December 1989 revolution. Through impromptu televised news conferences, the Front announced itself to the Romanian people and issued its first proclamations.

Genuine debate concerning policies and political personalities, however, was not facilitated by Romanian media prior to the election. Highly partisan newspapers and newsletters proliferated, but their coverage of events rarely distinguished between editorial content and news reporting. *Romania Libera,* which for years was the dutiful mouthpiece of the Socialist Democracy and Unity Front, offered some front-page "point/counterpoint" statements by Front and opposition spokesmen, and the paper's circulation expanded beyond 1 million.[12] But its editor, Petre Mihai Bacanu, grew closer to opposition parties and candidates as May 20 drew near, and the Front's leadership became increasingly doubtful of Bacanu's willingness to ensure what they thought was unbiased coverage.

Television and radio were also problematical. In Romania, one television and radio headquarters building in Bucharest housed studios, technical support facilities, and broadcast systems. Only a handful of staff were available for tasks ranging from camera operation, sound technicians, editing, etc. Sudden demands for access by dozens of political parties presented both Romanian Radio and Television and the Iliescu interim government with impossible dilemmas; to distribute air time equally among all competing parties would have meant production demands far outstripping available resources, while to select certain parties as deserving more attention would have subverted the democratic principles with which everyone wished to be associated.

In the end, the two months between the promulgation of an electoral law (mid March) and the election saw the state-owned radio and television broadcast short statements from any political party that prepared one, *read* on the air by the regular newscasters. These statements were in the form of programs and platforms, often laying out cloudy visions of Romania's past ills and future prospects.

Romanian Radio and Television did, however, undertake a number of interview programs in which principal candidates and party leaders were introduced to voters. A series called "Studio Electoral," for example, offered scores of brief introductory interviews where a reporter would ask general questions of candidates and allow them to describe both themselves and their political position.[13]

Perhaps most important was a two hour, forty-five minute debate featuring the three presidential candidates—Campeanu, Iliescu and Ratiu—on May 17. In this debate, which was extended beyond its scheduled length, each candidate was asked a variety of questions about the campaign and their policies if elected. The viewing audience encompassed perhaps three-quarters of all adult Romanians, and was conducted in a correct, if not cordial, atmosphere.[14]

In Romania's political landscape before the May 20 election, one ought not forget either the army or the Securitate that the army defeated in December. That the Romanian Army fought against Ceausescu was not surprising given Ceausescu's policies denying the armed forces the primary mission of national defense, instead increasing the army's economic role (construction, managing enterprises, etc.).[15] But the older echelon of the officer corps (including Iliescu's first defense minister, General Militaru who was seventy-four) intervened on December 22 not for "the people," but rather for the most palatable option—"establishment" figures like Iliescu. Younger officers found Militaru and the Front to be tardy in introducing democratic reforms within the army and in society generally. That General Victor A. Stanculescu was selected in February as the new defense minister did not quiet younger officers' concerns, and the continuance of these grievances affected negatively the army's reliability in mid-June 1990 disturbances. What the army will or will not do in politics, therefore, is a critical factor in defining the viability of an elected Romanian government.

Neither should we assume that the Securitate have been eliminated as a factor in present or future Romanian political struggles or unrest; their loyalty lies not with their executed benefactors, but rather with themselves. The thousands of Securitate who were not killed or captured (a total of perhaps 600 were either dead or in custody by the end of December, out of an estimated 10,000 to 20,000 full-time agents and functionaries) will remain a disquieting factor for years to come.[16] Prior to the May 20 vote, the FSN's failure to pursue vigorously the disbanding of the security establishment was another problem for Iliescu's legitimacy among the urban intelligentsia—that stratum most often confronted by Securitate intimidation in the Ceausescu years. Calls for the ouster of Internal Affairs Minister Mihai Ghitac were heard from February through May among angry throngs protesting in several major cities. Ghitac was also an issue in the February protests of junior army officers in Bucharest, demanding democratization more quickly.

All of these imposing obstacles to a Romanian democracy were exacerbated in early 1990 by the wretched economic condition of the country. By the late 1980s, Romania was impaled on rigid central planning, unyielding state ownership, and the devastating results of Ceausescu's singleminded effort to pay off foreign debt by wringing capital out of Romanians' living standard. There was nothing Iliescu could do prior to May elections in the way of economic reforms that would have generated any new hope; his appeal, by contrast, was that change under his leadership would not come so quickly that people would be denied one of the only secure aspects of their existence—a job.

Having noted these obstacles, however, there were nevertheless encouraging signs leading up to May 20. Iliescu, Roman and others who were visible members of the FSN's Executive Council did not comport themselves as dictators, and espoused from the outset values that would turn the country away from the totalitarianism of the past two or more decades. The Front's "socialist" orientation was evident as was the discomfort with a free play of critical ideas. After February 20–21 unrest in Bucharest involving threatening situations for interim government ministers, Iliescu referred to the need to punish "counterrevolutionaries"—characterizations too similar to the old establishment's view of any threat, and thus certain to enflame and deepen resentments. These were certainly not well chosen phrases, but did not imply a propensity towards lethal measures against protesters. Iliescu and Roman gave no evidence of being people who would themselves order mass killings as did the Ceausescu regime.

To the degree there was a public image of the Front's policy-orientation, then, it was as a left-of-center, quasi-socialist movement. In its Platform, the Front acknowledged the necessity of moving the country towards competitive politics and a market economy, but more slowly than the opposition.[17] The Front presented itself as a break from the communist past by people who had been communists, but had not supported either the anti-democratic Leninism of the Romanian Communist Party nor the megalomania of Nicolae Ceausescu.

For a substantial minority in Romania, especially the urban intelligentsia, the disavowal of their communist pasts by Iliescu, Roman and others was never enough. A document drafted in Timisoara on March 11, 1990—since known as the Timisoara Proclamation—demanded (in Article 8) that those politicians who had served as activists or security officers in past communist regimes should be barred from running as candidates in the election. Adoption of the Timisoara Proclamation became a theme of contention during the last month of the campaign.[18]

Important compromises were, however, reached during the spring of 1990 that cleared away some of the threatening obstacles to elections and a democratic transition. An electoral law drafted by the Front in February was opposed, and required negotiations that resulted in a March 14 promulgation of a complex electoral law (which, in fact, made the May 20th ballot extraordinarily difficult to understand). That the Front compromised on the electoral procedures while the opposition parties acquiesced on the issue of when the election ought to be held (the FSN arguing for an early vote so that the legitimation of an election could endow government with greater authority, while the other parties wanted a delayed election to give them more time to prepare), meant that some spirit of cooperation could be generated. Further, Iliescu had accepted the formation of a temporary Council of National Unity, in which the Front and thirty-seven other parties had a role, to operate as a de facto legislature until the convening of a parliament selected by the May elections. Half of this 253 member interim assembly was allocated to the Front, which itself became a matter of antagonism in Bucharest politics. But the Council of National Unity was, at least, a successful bridge during a crucial several months, avoiding both the appearance and any tendency towards a reassertion of one-party rule.

Electoral Outcomes

The National Salvation Front and interim President Ion Iliescu won a convincing victory on Sunday, May 20th. (See Table 1.)

Indictments of the FSN and Iliescu accompanied Western reports of the election.[19] In Romania, Ratiu and Campeanu alleged fraud, and spoke of not accepting the election results.[20] Charges and countercharges became increasingly heated in the last days of May and early days of June, as election observers' judgments were employed to support both the Front's contention that the vote was, by and large, fair and that incidents of intimidation or fraud were too infrequent and minor to have affected much of the outcome—*and* to underscore the opposition's assertion that there was "moral fraud" in the election.[21] Most observers, however, would agree with the assessment that the *campaign* was imperfect,

Romania's Perilous Path

TABLE 1   ROMANIAN ELECTORAL RESULTS

Presidential Election	% of Total	Vote Total
Ion Iliescu (National Salvation Front)	85.1	12,232,498
Radu Campeanu (Liberal)	10.2	1,529,188
Ion Ratiu (Peasants)	4.3	617,007

Lower House of Parliament (Assembly of Deputies)		
National Salvation Front	66.3	9,089,659
Hungarian Democratic Union of Romania	7.2	991,601
National Liberal Party	6.4	879,290
Romanian Ecological Movement	2.6	358,864
National Peasants Party	2.6	351,357
Romanian Unity Alliance--RUA	2.1	290,875
Agrarian Democratic Party	1.8	250,403
Romanian Ecological Party	1.7	232,212
Socialist Democratic Party	1.1	143,393
Other votes split among more than 50 parties		

Upper House (Senate) of Parliament		
National Salvation Front	67.0	9,353,006
Hungarian Democratic Union of Romania	7.2	1,004,353
National Liberal Party	7.1	985.094
National Peasant Party	2.5	348,687
Romanian Ecological Movement	2.45	341,478
Romanian Unity Alliance-RUA	2.15	300,473
Romanian Ecological Party	1.4	192,574
Other votes split among more than 50 parties		

SOURCE: B.A.C. (Central Electoral Bureau), May 25, 1990 as reported by the Rompres wire service on May 25, 1990. These data reflect the distribution after counting the 14,826,616 votes cast out of an estimated 17,200,722 eligible voters--a turnout rate of about 86%. There were 447,923 "invalid ballots".

including many incidents that endangered the opposition's capacity to mount a nationwide electoral effort. At the same time, election monitors acknowledged that the May 20th vote was generally clean.[22]

Notwithstanding accusations of fraud, one must recall that the FSN had moved resolutely, despite a situation of extraordinary difficulty, toward an election and its own role as a political competitor. In the aftermath of a violent uprising, the FSN assembled, and acted to ensure a statutory process. It accepted objections to its first draft electoral law and, by March 14, less than twelve weeks after the revolution, the electoral law was finalized.

Although one must rely on judgmental observations, there appears to be a strong aversion among Front leaders to recreate dictatorial or Leninist roles for themselves. Even if exercising such power were Iliescu or Roman's goal, they lack the institutional control necessary to effect such a goal. More important, they and their advisors do not have that inclination. At the top of the Front are engineers, economists and political scientists— pragmatic, and new to the game of mass politics. Their fault, and it is a considerable one, is to see as threatening those events that Greek, Spanish or Italian leaders regard as merely disruptive. Additionally, there is a tendency to be personally troubled by the notion that their qualifications and ethics are questioned in the aftermath of a popular mandate. Such a thin political skin harms their tolerance and willingness to be accepting of loud opponents and/or a critical foreign press, but does not make them indistinguishable from the Ceausescu dictatorship.

Iliescu and most of those around him were members of the Communist Party, and Iliescu had served as head of the Young Communist League in the late 1960s to 1971, and as First Party Secretary in a couple of counties (judete) in the early 1970s. But his break with Ceausescu had been *eighteen* years before the revolution and, although he had retained a post in the Communist Party hierarchy until the early 1980s, he had become an increasingly outspoken critic over the last decade. Further, Iliescu never filled the grey communist bureaucrat role; when I first met him in 1973, for example, Iliescu was a results-oriented local leader, who rolled up his shirtsleeves and spoke frankly.

Iliescu's past troubles many Romanians, and he knows it. His past, however, is an open book while, as Iliescu argues, his opponents in the presidential election also had checquered histories.[23] We should consider whether or not Front leaders' careers as Communist Party members require their condemnation in the same breath as Ceausescu. Iliescu and those around him repudiate the Ceausescu period without reservation and celebrate the revolution, many having been direct participants in December's fighting.

The Front's electoral opponents received 33% of the total vote for seats in the Chamber of Deputies (lower house), with the most successful opposition parties being the Hungarian Democratic Union at 7.6% and the National Liberals at 6.0%. (See Table 1.) The Peasants did not fare well, and drew no more votes than did the Romanian Ecological Movement (around 300,000—between 2 and 3% of the total). There were scores of other parties, movements and associations (including fifty-one that did not receive even 1% of all votes cast). The ones that counted most were the "historical" parties and the couple groupings, introduced earlier, that built on existing ethnonationalist or environmental concerns.

Student and urban-based opposition to the Front was evident and vocal during the months leading up to the election. Particularly in Bucharest and Timisoara, demonstrations were frequent from February through May. A core of perhaps several thousand, joined on May Day and on weekends by several times that number, regularly occupied Bucharest's central intersection—University Square—chanting slogans and singing protest songs. The demonstrators, many with links to and encouragement from opposition parties, indicted Iliescu for his Communist Party past, and equated him with the Ceausescu period. The Front generally was criticized as having made a pact with the Securitate, and Iliescu as participating in a conspiracy to steal the revolution and maintain the secret police in power.

In this kind of environment, it was nothing short of amazing that anything resembling a fair election occurred in Romania.

Post-Electoral Unrest and Western Responses

Romania is, after Ceausescu's overthrow and execution, no longer a tyranny. But, as events in mid-June sadly demonstrated, it is also a long way from being a democracy. Somewhere in between, with the shadow of Ceausescu grimly evident, is a Romania struggling against all odds to find a new political equilibrium.

What happened in Bucharest in mid-June was, in one sense, predictable. Some governments, including democracies with a long track record, might resolve to retake the capital city's central square from demonstrators who had occupied it for two months. And, in a country where tolerance of those who protest, and trust in those with power are both rare commodities, every issue becomes volatile, compromise is impossible, and violence from both sides a likely response.

President Ion Iliescu, Prime Minister Petre Roman, and their advisors had discussed the need to move protesters out of the University Square in April. In their discussions in late April and early May, it was not the presence of Western election monitors at that time that prevented action (as inferred by some of the U.S. press). Neither was it their departure that enabled Iliescu to take action. Rather, a decision was made to wait and see if, after the May 20 election, the protestors would accept the results and disband gradually and quietly.

They did not. Instead, the issue of the Square's occupation heated up, with clashing viewpoints being expressed in publications of principal parties. In the Front's *Adevarul* there was comment about the "futility" of a "dictatorship of the streets,"[24] while the opposition *Dreptatea*[25] published a comment by the National Council of People's Alliance demanding an expansion of demonstrations and *Romania Libera,* just prior to the election, included the "Declaration" of University Square protesters.[26] Meanwhile, rumors spread about plans on both sides—for the protesters to attack government buildings or for the army to move against the demonstration.

No doubt against the advice of many advisors—some of whom clearly advocated waiting out the protesters indefinitely—Iliescu ordered the uniformed police to clear University Square on the night of June 13th. Because of these arrests, and the rough physical treatment by police, the following day and night saw thousands of protestors attack principal government targets such as the headquarters of Romanian Radio and Television, the police headquarters, the foreign ministry (where Iliescu maintained his office) and other sites. Army troops at these sites apparently resorted to gunfire on several occasions, and several people were killed.

As viewed from the windows of the foreign ministry building, there must have been a number of hours when it seemed as if the government that had just been elected by over 80% of the population was about to be overthrown. It was later argued by Dr. Ion Pascu, a close advisor to Iliescu, that the army was slow to respond to the government's appeals for more troops to restore order, and that the regular police were nowhere to be found.

Iliescu's "control" of key institutions such as the army, police and bureaucracy is very limited. In early May, I heard from the National Salvation Front leadership in Bucharest that it was unable to direct or discipline people in the provinces who said that they were affiliated with the Front. Further, the national and local bureaucracies were almost untouchable until a legitimating election occurred. The Romanian Army, of course, had fought Ceausescu's Securitate once (in December), and very likely has little inclination to confront university students and others. The army is, moreover, stretched very thinly given the peacekeeping function it now fills in areas of mixed Hungarian/Romanian population in Transylvania. It (the army) is neither well-armed nor well-disciplined. Defense Minister Stanculescu probably conveyed to Iliescu that, beyond defending key governmental buildings, civic order would have to be the Government's task.

That Iliescu issued an appeal for citizens' defense of the government is thus explicable if not excusable. Industrial workers, including miners, are one stratum in which Iliescu has had unswerving support. Iliescu is personally popular in the countryside and factories. Communist pasts do not bother most Romanian workers, but the fear of unemployment does—and the Front gained workers' allegiance by guaranteeing slow economic transitions towards a market economy. Further, there is no love lost between workers and urban intelligentsia in Romania—an old class division that the communist period did absolutely nothing to dispel. When the miners heard Iliescu's appeal, there was little doubt that they would respond, and do so with violent abandon.

Romania's Perilous Path 87

The "excesses" of the several thousand miners were more than that. The attacks on opposition party headquarters and homes of politicians were reprehensible. A test of the Iliescu government will be if, and how vigorously, any investigation is pursued of their rampage through Bucharest.

Were the miners directed by the Securitate, and is Iliescu in league with the resurgent secret police? The truth is neither yes nor no. Iliescu, Roman and those immediately around him are by no means covert Securitate survivors. They all lived through a period dominated by Ceausescu's secret police, and do not want a return of such an environment. Yet, we ought not doubt that the Securitate will try to take advantage of unrest, exacerbate violence, and discredit politicians of all stripes who wish to move Romania away from its past tyranny.

Another test for Iliescu, and one that will be a measure of his and Roman's commitment to a democratic environment, will be the degree to which he tries to identify and prosecute remaining Securitate operatives throughout the bureaucracy, army, and socioeconomic organizations of the country.

These events were not a conspiracy hatched by Iliescu to create an excuse for a crackdown. He was urged to wait to act against the University Square occupation, the hope being that it would dissipate on its own. The action taken against the protesters was by the police, at night, to minimize the potential for angry reactions—after which the government was unable to rely on the army or the police. Fearful of its own downfall, the government called on an organized, reliable—and violent—element of industrial labor.

This, then, was the action of a nervous government that does not know—and may never learn—the language and behavior of a tolerant, plural democracy. We should, however, not forget that Iliescu was elected in a reasonably correct vote after a campaign that ought to have been more perfect, but was far more open than anything Romania had known for fifty years. As a consequence of their overwhelming victory, Iliescu and Roman think they have a mandate and *expect* to govern without challenges to their legitimacy.

Iliescu *should* have, had he decided on the basis of our values, let the University Square occupation go on; it was costing him, the National Salvation Front, and the country relatively little. His action against protesters was a consequence of a threat perception characteristic of people unaccustomed to the cacophony of democracies. His government was then besieged by Western criticism.[27] Chances of a constructive dialogue with opposition parties were irrevocably damaged, and the electoral legitimacy gained on May 20 was weakened. Romania's prognosis, and democracy's chances, were not helped by these events.

Conclusion

Romania's election produced a mandate for the FSN, but it neither assured the Front of institutional control nor legitimacy among a critical stratum of the population—the urban intelligentsia. Without the latter two elements of political authority, the government of President Ion Iliescu and Prime Minister Roman will be confronted by repeated challenges.

Steps to inaugurate economic reform, and to bring into principal government posts a wide variety of respected individuals, have been taken.[28] But these actions, without developing means by which to effect its authority throughout the state apparatus and educated elite, may be ephemeral. As large as the FSN victory was, May 20th elections provided little in the way of political security for this first post-Ceausescu government.

Notes

1. Among the negative assessments of the FSN as a recapitulation of the Ceausescu period was Vladimir Tismaneanu in "New Masks, Old Faces: The Romanian Junta's Familiar Look," *The New Republic* (February 5, 1990).

2. Sergiu Chelac, Conversation with Author, Washington, D.C. (February, 1990).

3. "Comunicatul catre Tara al Consiliului Frontului Salvarii Nationale," *Curierul Romanesc,* Anul 1, Nr. 1 (December 31, 1989)

4. "Demonstrators Seize Romanian Deputy Premier," *Financial Times* (February 19, 1990).

5. Several initial accounts of political parties and groups that emerged in Romania are informative. For brief summaries, see *East European Newsletter,* Vol. 4, No. 1 (January 8, 1990).

6. Vladimir Volodin, "With Liberals on Balcescu Boulevard," *Izvestiya* (January 26, 1990).

7. "Romanian Election Campaign Marred by Violent Attacks Against Opposition," *Radio Free Europe (RFE) Report,* Vol. VII, No. 31 (May 20, 1990), pp. 3–4; also see, Dan Ionescu, "Violence and Calumny in the Election Campaign," Radio Free Europe, *Report on Eastern Europe,* Vol. 1, No. 21 (May 25, 1990), pp. 37–41.

8. International Human Rights Law Group (IHRL), News Release on presidential and legislative elections in Romania (May 14, 1990).

9. See, for example, *Dreptatea* (May 9, 1990), p. 1; also see Irina de Chikoff, Interview with Radu Campeanu, *Le Figaro* (May 8, 1990), p. 3.

10. The official Romanian government account, and the provisional leadership's promise to establish a special commission to investigate these events, were conveyed in "Comunicatul catre Tara al Consiliului Frontului Salvarii Nationale," *Curierul Romanesc,* Anul 1, Nr. 1 (December 31, 1989).

11. Budapest Domestic Service Broadcast, May 18, 1990 translated in Foreign Broadcast Information Service (FBIS) *Daily Report: Eastern Europe* 90-099 (May 22, 1990), p. 47.

12. Celestine Bohlen, "Showcase for Bucharest's Dissenters," *New York Times* (February 1, 1990), p. 14.

13. Bucharest Domestic Service Broadcast, June 2, 1990 translated in Foreign Broadcast Information Service (FBIS) *Daily Report: Eastern Europe* 90-107 (June 4, 1990), p. 53.

14. Jacques Boyer, "Iliescu Dominates Electoral Debate," Agence France Press (AFP) dispatch (May 18, 1990).

15. Daniel N. Nelson, "Ceausescu and the Romanian Army," *International Defense Review*, Vol. 22, No. 6 (September, 1989).

16. Daniel N. Nelson, Interviews with President Iliescu and presidential advisors in Bucharest (late April–early May, 1990).

17. Frontul Salvarii Nationale, *Platforma Program* (Bucharest: FSN, 1990).

18. Contrast, for example, Florin-Gabriel Marculescu, "Articol 8," *Romania Libera* (April 26, 1990), p. 3; also see Darie Novaceanu's commentary in *Adevarul* (May 8, 1990), p. 1.

19. See, for instance, Nora Boustany, "State Department Says Elections in Romania Were Tainted," *Washington Post* (May 26, 1990).

20. Rompres Dispatch, May 21, 1990, "Will Mr. Ratiu Contest the Elections?," translated in Foreign Broadcast Information Service (FBIS) *Daily Report: Eastern Europe* 90-099 (May 22, 1990), p. 37. Also see Bucharest Domestic Service Broadcast, op. cit., (May 22, 1990), pp. 37–38, and (May 24, 1990), p. 67.

21. Contrast the FSN's Views expressed by Julian Constandache in *Tineretul Liber* (May 22, 1990), p. 1 with those of Iliescu's critics such as Octavian Paler in *Romania Libera* (May 29, 1990), pp. 1–2.

22. Rompres Dispatch, May 22, 1990, "Elections in Romania: Observers' Opinions—. . . There Were Irregularities But They Could Not Have A Decisive Influence" and "British Group: The Elections Were Fair," reprinted in Foreign Broadcast Information Service (FBIS) *Daily Report: Eastern Europe* 90-100 (May 23, 1990), pp. 48–49.

23. See Sylvie Kauffman's interview with Ion Iliescu in *Le Monde* (May 17, 1990), p. 3.

24. *Adevarul* (May 23, 1990), pp. 1, 3.

25. *Dreptatea* (May 27, 1990) p. 1.

26. "Declaratie," *Romania Libera* (May 18, 1990), pp. 1, 5.

27. For example, "Romania's Stalinists," *Washington Post*, Editorial (June 17, 1990).

28. Judy Dempsey, "Romania Paves Way for Market Economy and Privatisation," *Financial Times* (June 29, 1990).

5

Turkish Uncertainties: Domestic and Foreign Policy Identities in the 1990s

Introduction

Seventy years ago, Turkey's great nationalist hero of the modern era, Mustafa Kemal Ataturk, battled to establish an independent Turkish republic committed to a European-oriented path of modernization. Ataturk was no democrat, but his was a vision of unity and greatness that Turkey still longs to achieve. The homage paid to Ataturk even today stems, in large part, from his unfulfilled aspirations for his country.

In the 1990s and beyond, critical issues confront Turkey—at the core of which is the nation's identity expressed in domestic politics and foreign policy. In the balance rests the well-being of Turkey's rapidly increasing population, and quite possibly the balance of power between Western democracies or radical Islamic interests in the Eastern Mediterranean.

Domestic Policies

One image of Turkey is that of a cosmopolitan Istanbul and high-fashion coastal regions where Turkey's European identity was decided long ago. But orientations are quite different in village Turkey. Although urbanization is rapid, half of the country's population remains in the countryside, a fact quickly forgotten in the dense traffic and crowded shopping areas of Istanbul (with almost seven million inhabitants) and Ankara (perhaps three and a half million).

In rural areas, Islamic fundamentalism became a strong force in the 1980s, challenging the secular principles that Ataturk had enunciated, and giving rise to Necmettin Erbakan's "Welfare Party" which adopts anti-American, anti-European rhetoric in the name of Islam. Although the party has been banned from an open electoral challenge, its popularity is symptomatic of a strong undercurrent of Turkish sentiment that is disinclined to further "Europeanize" behavior or laws in their country, and wants less not more contact with the West. Emphasis on Islam and the Koran have been promoted by funding from Iran and other Islamic states, and particularly in Eastern Anatolia the building of mosques is a clear sign of such investment.[1]

The prognosis for Turkish democracy is interwoven with Islamic fundamentalism as well. Quite simply, will a competitive democracy survive and become strengthened during the 1990s, or will a combination of separatist/fundamentalist violence and military countermeasures bring democratic institutions to their knees?

In 1960 and again in 1980, the Turkish Army effected coups and instituted martial law. Domestic violence mounted in the late 1970s during the term of Prime Minister Suleyman Demirel and his Justice Party, as leftist and rightist organizations among students, workers and other strata fought battles that left thousands dead each year. The army's 1980 coup was welcomed by many Turks not because of pro-military sentiments but because of the relief that the army takeover brought from escalating violence. It is clear that the Turkish military, once it ousts a particular political leadership and system, is not interested in occupying formal governmental roles for very long. Both in 1960 and 1980, civilians were returned to power in new elections within a year or two.

The army, however, retains a watchful eye on civilian political developments, and is never far removed from power. Indeed, as a senior member of Parliament told me, the "army's budget is whatever the army says it must be"—and the Parliament lacks the capacity to alter the allocation of resources in any way that would affect the military. It is no surprise, of course, that the Turkish General Staff has such power; the constitution of November 1982 was written with a military veto over any unacceptable provisions, and the first post-coup election in 1983 took place under a ban imposed on the political activity of one hundred politicians who the military identified as destabilizing or subversive—including former Prime Ministers Bulent Ecevit and Suleyman Demirel.

Although mainstream parties have had unrestrained participation in recent elections, the Turkish United Communist Party is still banned as are a variety of other extremist parties (e.g., the Welfare Party of Islamic fundamentalists, a neo-fascist National Work Party and others). It was not until early 1990 that Haydar Kutlu and Nihat Sargin, who had been arrested in November 1987 upon re-entry into Turkey from exile in Western Europe, were finally set free. Turkey remains one of the very few countries in Europe to maintain absolute prohibitions on the political activity of either extreme.[2]

Elections in November 1987 resulted in the continued rule of the centrist Motherland Party (ANAP) and its Western-oriented leader, Turgut Ozal, who remained prime minister. With 290 seats in the 450 seat Parliament, Ozal could not claim a mandate, but was able to retain control. Elections were widely seen as free and devoid of troublesome irregularities, although the electoral system disadvantages minority parties that may receive only slightly smaller proportions of the popular vote, but wind up getting only 15% of the parliamentary seats. By contrast, the Motherland Party received just 35% of the vote but gained almost two thirds of the National Assembly seats. A 10% minimum popular vote further disqualified four of six opposition parties from receiving *any* parliamentary seats, in effect disenfranchising many voters.

By a year later, however, Ozal's popularity had plummeted. Poor economic performance (inflation and slow growth) plus suspicion that Ozal was trying to create a family dynasty had greatly undermined his base of support.[3] According to some public opinion polls by late summer 1989, fewer than one in five Turks thought highly of Ozal. A year later, ANAP was receiving only about 15% in random surveys of voters—that is, a poor third behind both principal opposition parties.[4]

Given these mounting political difficulties, the Motherland Party's poor showing in local elections, and rumors of his own deteriorating health, Ozal gave up the prime minister post to become president on November 9, 1989, when President (and former General) Kenan Evren's term ended. Ozal's election by Parliament was not easy and, indeed, took several ballots. The True Path Party (conservatives) led by Demirel and the Social Democrat Populist Party (SHP) led by Erdal Inonu boycotted the parliamentary vote, and Ozal's election was by a narrow margin.[5] Replacing Ozal as prime minister is Yildirim Akbulut, known to be loyal to ANAP and obedient to Ozal. The press, however, has not been impressed by the new prime minister, and the disdain for him may lead to an early departure. Meanwhile, Ozal has turned the previously ceremonial presidency into a truly executive office, largely displacing the prime minister in day-to-day governance.

But it should be noted that the popularity of specific politicians, the electoral system and even the army's proclivity to intervene in politics are not the weakest links of Turkish democracy. Instead, there remains a broad lack of public and elite confidence in the ability of democracy to perform well—to, indeed, ensure the well-being of the nation. That sentiment, which combines impatience, doubt, and genuine concern, is fueled by severe economic difficulties which accelerated during the last half of the 1980s.

Inflation, throughout 1989 and 1990, was at least 70% and unemployment hovered around 15%. Estimates of lower and higher rates are often cited, since data are imprecise, and calculations depend on methodology and time period being considered. Nevertheless, the Ozal government and to some degree the current political system are taking the heat, as it were, for rapidly deteriorating purchasing power and expanding inequalities among socioeconomic strata.

Ozal as prime minister was seen by the opposition, and many in his own party as well, as a free spender. He has been characterized as someone who, in the name of economic growth, jettisoned price controls, privatized much of the country's industry and lifted import restrictions. Beginning in 1989, Turkey *did* show a balance of payment surplus, yet domestic demand is so overheated that inflation remains at dangerous levels while budget deficits are very large (around 4% of GDP). Debt is now around $37 billion, which is large, indeed, for a country with a per capita income of not much more than $1300 per year. As long as the current account runs a surplus (as it did in 1988 through 1990), Turkey will meet its debt commitments. But critics of ANAP policies ask at what price Turkey is meeting these obligations. Ozal's economic policies, pleasing to the IMF, the EC and to the United States, have the taint of bowing before Western demands—demands beyond which was supposed to be the "reward" of European Community (EC) membership that, by December 1989, was put on hold by the EC.

With the economic picture looking bleak for many Turks, and the government's image tarnished by the failure to achieve greater status vis-à-vis Europe while adopting many economic steps demanded by the EC, the Motherland Party's support, and Ozal's popularity, are at low ebb. An attempted assassination on June 18, 1988, as he was addressing Parliament gave Ozal a temporary boost from sympathy, but economic issues and emerging scandals (especially the Horzum case, otherwise known as the Emlak Bank scandal) from late 1988 into the fall of 1989 made Ozal's departure from the prime ministership virtually a necessity. ANAP and Ozal have been unable to avoid the indictment by Inonu's Social Democrats for having failed to guard "national integrity."

Whether Turkey will continue on the path towards full engagement in Europe and whether its democracy will remain intact are mutually dependent processes. The West, and the U.S. specifically, cannot determine the outcome of these critical issues, but it is clear where the interests of America and the EC lie. NATO allies can alter the external environment by providing to Turkey both more of the tangible benefits (markets for exports, for example) and intangible attention that such a key state warrants. The West can, as well, provide the maximum latitude for Ankara to extract itself from severe inflation and underdevelopment via further renegotiation of loans and continued aid and assistance.

Neither the United States nor Europe, however, can decide for Turkey how to ensure the integrity of a competitive democracy, free from the peril of both political violence and military intervention. None of Turkey's friends can resolve the impasse of secularism versus Islamic fundamentalism, and aid from the West will never substitute for Turkey's own commitment to Ataturk's vision of a developed, progressive Turkey. In these respects, the political future of Turkey rests not with American or European "fixes" for domestic challenges, but on the talent of today's Turkish leaders and resolve of its people.

Turkey and Strategic Realignment

Turks, Russians and warfare—for centuries, these were virtually synonymous. The Ottoman and Russian empires alternately ruled over and fought for, each others' territory and peoples from the Balkans to Central Asia, with the Black Sea and Caucasus often in the midst of battle.[6]

Never have Turks and Russians been on the same side in war, notwithstanding Ataturk's flirtation with the pre-Stalin Bolshevik regime in the 1920s and Turkish neutrality in World War II. Hostility between the two nations has been long and fierce, and this history irrevocably weighs heavily on present dynamics in the strategic region that joins Europe and the Middle East. At the confluence of the Eastern Mediterranean, few bilateral relations not involving two major economic or military actors are suffused with such importance.

Matters of Security

The Turkish republic of today retains a healthy suspicion of Moscow. When civilian government returned to Turkey in 1983, expectations for better relations with the Soviets did not occur immediately. Both because of the military's still strong influence in Turkish politics and because of the leadership interregnum in the USSR, both Ankara and Moscow fell back on old slogans and antipathies during the early to mid 1980s.

As Turks look north from the Bosporus now, however, the view of both Soviet reality and their own security has begun to change in significant ways. Turkey's relations with the USSR have, in fact, shifted into new uncharted territory. Changes within the USSR wrought by Mikhail Gorbachev's reforms, the pragmatism of centrist civilian leadership in Ankara, the continuing power of Islamic fundamentalism, and other more imminent security issues confronting Turkey (such as Iraqi aggression against Kuwait) are the propellants for such movement.

Just how disquieting that shift might be to NATO was suggested in May 1989. On May 20th of that year, Turkey's political and military leadership found themselves with a Soviet defector—not unusual, except for the way he arrived.[7] Flying his Mig-29 Fulcrum to a civilian airfield in eastern Turkey—perhaps the best plane in the Soviet air force and the pride of its air defense system—Captain Aleksandr Zuyev provided an unparalleled opportunity to examine the USSR's recent advances in aircraft construction, avionics and armaments.

The Turks, however, refused to delay the return of the Mig-29 to the USSR by Soviet personnel, denying to the United States what would have been in 1989 an intelligence goldmine. Although some Turkish examination of the aircraft did take place in the thirty hours it remained on Turkish soil, even a personal plea from the then-chairman of the joint chiefs of staff, Admiral Crowe, to General Necip Torumtay, chief of staff of the Turkish military, failed to change Ankara's position.

At the Pentagon and in corridors of other NATO ministries of defense, the Turkish action seemed at the least, ill-considered given Turkey's keen desire to join fully the Europe that still holds Ankara somewhat at arms length. At worst, it was a serious breach of the mutual expectations among NATO allies. Although later reports based on interviews with Turkish military officers suggest that a great deal of use to NATO *was* learned by metallurgical and electronic analysis, the absence of U.S. (or British) personnel made the Turkish examination less helpful than it might have been.

Such a refusal to cooperate fully on a matter of security was, however, quite consistent with then prime minister, now President Turgut Ozal's earnest effort to avoid "international ramifications" with the USSR. Although the Turkish Foreign Ministry rationalized the Mig-29 decision by emphasizing its desire to refrain from disrupting the lessening of tensions in Europe, treading softly vis-à-vis Moscow is based on assessments that imminent threats to Turkey have not originated in the USSR for some time.

Readjusting threat assessments and, broadly, their understanding of security has been an ongoing process among Turkish political, military and academic elites for the past decade and a half—dating principally from the U.S. arms embargo following Turkey's invasion of Cyprus. But the motivation for Ankara's security reassessments has deep roots.

At the end of World War II, Turkey was embraced by the United States as part of a strategy of containment, and became a member of *both* NATO (in 1952) and a founding member of the now-defunct CENTO. Turkey became a forward-deployment for American listening posts, air bases, and (in the late 1950s) our earliest intermediate-range ballistic missiles. For Turks, the immediate post-war period had evoked an ominous specter of Stalinist expansionism, with Soviet troops occupying northwestern Iran, the Red Army thoroughly in control in

Turkish Uncertainties 97

Bulgaria and Romania, and a communist insurgency in Greece. In such circumstances, Turkish and American interest coincided.

These U.S. bases are still critical to American security and NATO intelligence capabilities. Their modernization, for instance, was a diplomatic and economic issue between Washington and Ankara during the mid-1980s; after a 3-½-year wait, the U.S. is now up-dating computer and radar at the Pirinclik and Belbasi monitoring stations that gather data on Soviet nuclear explosions and military activities. The airbase at Sinop on the Black Sea Coast, used primarily as Turkey's radar intelligence center with American personnel closely involved, is also being updated.

These vital facilities help to bind the West to Turkey and vice-versa. This close association with NATO has meant that Turks have been a critical anchor for the alliance's Southern Command and contribute disproportionately to NATO's total manpower. Indeed, with the second largest military in NATO (roughly 800,000 in the active duty armed forces), with continuous and costly efforts to modernize forces (e.g., the assembly of 160 F-16s in Turkey) and with military expenditures as a proportion of GNP among the highest in the alliance (at 4.9% behind only the U.S. and Greece), it is difficult for NATO councils to deny the substantial contribution of Turkey to collective defense for the past several decades.[8]

Yet, this very closeness in terms of military cooperation enhanced the Turkish expectation that they will be taken seriously and treated equally in their economic and political relations with Western Europe and the United States. There is a public, academic and governmental conviction that the country's sacrifice on behalf of NATO's southern flank throughout the Cold War should have been recognized and that compensatory steps ought to have been implemented. Such compensation would, in the Turkish view, include much greater access for Turkey's exports (textiles, fruits, and manufactured items) in Western markets in order to reduce Ankara's trade deficit with developed market economies. Further, the wealthier NATO members, especially the U.S. and Germany, ought to provide larger amounts of aid, and that aid should be in the form of *grants,* not credits, loans and technical assistance. American security assistance to Turkey has totaled well above half a billion dollars annually, placing Ankara behind only countries such as Israel, Egypt and Pakistan in recent years. Nevertheless, one hears vociferous complaints in Ankara and Istanbul that this is far less than Turkey needs and is due.

More than the security assistance issue alone, however, the enmity between Greece and Turkey affects negatively Ankara's ties with the West. From the Turkish perspective, the Greek socialist government (PASOK) of Andreas Papandreou acted provocatively towards Turkey, and Prime Minister Mitsotakis is also off to a bad start. Ankara cites as evidence various maritime incidents on the Aegean Sea, confrontations in the airspace over the sea and its thousands of islands and, increasingly, alleged Greek attacks on ethnic Turks in Western Thrace.[9]

Further, Turks point to the January 1985 announcement from Athens of a new military policy that identified Turkey as Greece's principal threat, and redeployed Greek forces accordingly. A September 1986 Greek-Bulgarian Protocol of Friendship and Cooperation is cited by the Turks as a major step in heightening regional tensions, and military and government officials express indignation at the lack of NATO condemnation of such an accord. The electoral losses of Papandreou's party in June 1989, and the establishment of the Mitsotakis government in the Spring of 1990, enabled Turkey to hope for some improvement in relations; neither the Greek conservatives nor Turks, however, have become less intransigent about Cyprus and other disputes.

Turkish military leaders note, as well, their cooperation with the U.S. on basing and intelligence gathering facilities which intercept a large proportion of all signal intelligence collected on the USSR by American agencies, while the Greeks have made life very difficult for the U.S. Helinikon Air Base, outside Athens, is soon to close, and discussions about bases on Crete such as Souda Bay were difficult and protracted. Meanwhile, the Turks complain bitterly that American military assistance is tied to levels provided to Greece by, in Ankara's view, the "infamous" 7:10 ratio—followed by the U.S. Congress since the Foreign Relations Act of 1960 stipulated such a ratio to maintain "the current balance of military strength" between Greece and Turkey. Although the U.S. arms embargo, imposed in 1975 after the Turks invaded Cyprus, was lifted long ago, military and governmental officials in Ankara retain their view that a "Greek lobby" could once again lead America to abandon Turkey were there a conflict with Greece.

Turkish ire was also raised by the October 1989 resolution of the U.S. Senate that honored Armenians killed by Ottoman Turks from 1915–1923. The resolution was passed in the Senate's Judiciary Committee, and was sponsored by Senator Robert Dole. Reacting angrily to the passage of such a resolution, the Turkish government notified the U.S. of sanctions to be imposed against U.S. military facilities, denying to American aircraft and naval units a number of facilities to which they regularly have access.[10]

By comparison, frictions with Bulgaria, the origins of which lie in ex-Bulgarian Communist Party (BCP) leader Todor Zhivkov's disastrous policy of forced assimilation of ethnic Turks, brought neither greater Turkish reliance on ties with NATO nor worsened relations with the USSR. To the contrary, Turkey's concerns about Bulgaria have been directed towards the USSR. The Soviets were asked to condemn Zhivkov's

Turkish Uncertainties

policies and to dampen tensions and to urge change in BCP policies. Although this was never any explicit condemnation, Gorbachev was supportive—if not more—of Zhivkov's November 1989 ouster. The USSR is thus viewed as potentially cooperative vis-à-vis punitive American actions when Turkish interests clash with Greece. The "bottom-line" to Ankara is quite simple: NATO and the U.S. in particular are blamed for failing to modify Greek behavior, while Moscow is credited with attempting to modify provocative Bulgarian policies.

As of early 1989, Turks accounted for between 10–15% of Bulgaria's 9.4 million people, depending on estimates of the ethnic Turks (under 1.0 million according to Bulgarian government accounts, 1.4 million in Turkish sources). There are, in addition, a couple hundred thousand ethnic Bulgarian Moslems who have faced many of the same constraints on personal liberties, not to mention a large Gypsy minority. Zhivkov and other BCP opponents of social or political change began in 1984 to implement policies that insisted on the use of Bulgarian surnames, prohibited the use of the Turkish language for instruction or media broadcasts, restricted Turkish-language publications, and impeded the practice of Islam through closing of mosques.

This effort to create, forcibly if necessary, a "single socialist nation" without ethnic identity other than Bulgarian, was bound to fail. During 1984–1985, a number of violent incidents including the bombing of trains and train stations were reported. Other violent encounters between Turkish/Moslem protesters and security police or militia units may have cost many more lives, with Turkish authorities claiming that 1,000 people had died. These deaths temporarily suppressed the overt turmoil in regions where ethnic Turks have a sizeable presence—along the southern border of Bulgaria with Greece and Turkey, and in the northeast of the country, bordering Romania and the Black Sea.

In 1989, these regions again exhibited widespread protest demonstrations, strikes, and fighting between Turks and the authorities. Units of the Bulgarian People's Army may have been involved in crushing some of the demonstrations, and *Rabotnichesko Delo* (the BCP daily at that time) reported seven deaths and twenty-five injured.[11] Outside reports noted estimates as high as 30. As demonstration leaders, their families and many others were expelled from Bulgaria, panic set in among ethnic Turks, leading to an exodus of over 300,000 people, most being uprooted without reimbursement for property and possessions left behind. Many cases of family separations because of deportation were documented, adding to human suffering and to Turkey's visceral reaction.

For Turkey, the treatment of their ethnic counterparts in Bulgaria, and the significant burden of hundreds of thousands of Turkish refugees, became issues of national pride as well as matters useful in domestic politics. Political parties in Turkey sought whatever political advantage possible from tensions with Bulgaria, and Ozal, who had been so badly damaged by electoral outcomes and scandal that his resignation was thought to be possible earlier in 1989, found it impossible to resist the nationalism espoused by some of his principal allies in the Motherland Party. Moscow was seen, by Ozal, Foreign Minister Yilmaz and General Turumtay as the only power which could engender some modification of Bulgarian policy. Although vilifying Bulgaria generally has been politically popular in Turkey, and has aroused substantial public furor, there has surely been no desire for an eruption of armed clashes between forces of the two countries among principal Turkish leaders. Instead, there has been, particularly in 1989, considerable fear that public militancy will outpace anything that can be done short of war.

Requests for Moscow's intervention were made by the Turks, and the Soviets apparently initiated discussions, through their embassy in Sofia and in Moscow, with Bulgarian officials up to the level of foreign minister—i.e., Petar Mladenov in the spring and summer 1989.[12] Although the content of these consultations is not known, one can surmise that Gorbachev and Shevardnadze sought a way for Zhivkov or a successor BCP leader to retain social control without unbridled coercion. By November, Gorbachev had made his desire known that Zhivkov be removed.

But, of course, any formula for reduced tension will eventually have to include an orderly process for the emigration of ethnic Turks—a process that might lessen protest within Turkish regions of Bulgaria, diminish the economic disruption of such a large departure from the Bulgarian workforce, and save face for a Turkish government that may again confront popular demands for confrontation with Bulgaria. Achieving such a diplomatic way out for both sides, however, depends largely on the willingness and capacity of the Soviets to "lean" on the long-time sycophants in Sofia. The post-communist leadership remains dependent on the USSR, but Moscow's capacity for any external crisis intervention has become questionable.

In other matters of Turkish security, the distances between positions of Moscow and Ankara have also diminished. Islamic fundamentalism is of no small concern to the urban elites of Istanbul, Ankara and Mediterranean/Aegean coasts. Already, the secular heritage that Ataturk established for twentieth century Turkey has run headlong into Islamic traditions such as head-coverings for female students at universities and other educational institutions. Turkish law forbids such religious displays, while Islamic fundamentalists demand that their religious law be followed.[13] Relations between Iran and Turkey, indeed, were disrupted by this issue far more than by the nine years of the Gulf War.

Turkish Uncertainties

Yet, the Turkish civilian and military leadership has begun to recognize a kind of secular alliance among states on the periphery of Islamic fundamentalism and radicalism. Although Moslems within the USSR are still under 20% of the total population, Central Asia and republics such as Azerbaijan are predominantly Islamic, and are experiencing rapid population growth rates. Both political systems will try to strike their own bargains with domestic Islamic fundamentalists, but strong elements of shared concern have arisen in the late 1980s where it did not exist before.

Likewise, the ethnic separatism of Kurds, and violent attacks mounted by the PKK organization in Eastern Anatolia, are issues of security that pushes Ankara away from NATO and towards closer ties with Russian leadership. To some NATO and EC members, the Kurds are an oppressed minority, forcibly assimilated in much the same way as ethnic Turks have suffered in Bulgaria. The Turks were not pleased, for example, by the omission of the PKK from a U.S. Department of Defense/State Department publication on terrorist organizations in late 1988.[14] The Soviets, however, now confront a growing list of independence-minded national fronts and heightened levels of violence liberally laced with nationalistic sentiment.

And, even before the Iraqi attack on Kuwait and the ensuing international crisis in 1990, no military or security planner in Ankara could forget that Iraq has a military even larger than Turkey's. Saddam Hussein's substantial and battle-tested chemical warfare and missile-firing capabilities were made all the more threatening by Iraq's re-built nuclear facilities (now dispersed to preclude another successful Israeli air attack) and the implied capability to very soon produce atomic weapons.[15] Although Turkey managed to remain on relatively good terms with Baghdad during the Gulf War—allowing the shipment of Iraqi oil to Turkish ports through a pipeline built for that purpose—no one in the Turkish General Staff is sanguine about the border with Iraq. To the south, a heavily armed Syria, with a high degree of volatility whenever Assad departs from the political landscape, also cannot be ignored.

Perhaps neither erstwhile superpower can protect Turkey's southern flank. But only the USSR can claim to have substantial political and military influence with these states on Turkey's eastern and southern borders. Ankara can expect no significant intervention from the East and any U.S. support for Turkey vis-à-vis the radical Arab world, from Ankara's perspective, might be counterproductive.

The real, the tangible or the immediate threats to Turkish security thus appear generated from other than the longstanding NATO adversary: "Turkey's main perception of military threat is neither the Soviet Union nor the East bloc. It is the eastern neighbors of Turkey"[16] This threat is mitigated not by NATO or the U.S. Indeed, the U.S.-Iraqi confrontation, from Ankara's perspective, may appear to have considerably heightened the level of threat to Turkey. The Greek-Turkish enmity continues to drive a wedge between Turkey and the rest of NATO as does the related matter of security assistance. The events involving ethnic Turks in Bulgaria have been politically useful to President Ozal's Motherland Party—to a point. In 1989, Turkish military and civilian authorities sought Soviet aid to pressure Zhivkov to modify policies directed against ethnic Turks. Later, Soviet emissaries were used to try to convince the new Lukanov government in Sofia to steer clear of closer ties to Greece. That such links are being enhanced anyway does not diminish other Turkish security concerns about which neither the U.S. or NATO can act effectively. Indeed, the affinity of Turkish and Soviet positions on some issues—Islamic fundamentalism, ethnic separatism, and human rights—plus the greater influence of Moscow in Baghdad and Damascus, underscore the importance of Turkey's links with the USSR.

When Turks made security-related choices in the last half of the 1980s, and into 1990, then, care has been taken to open lines of communication and commerce with the USSR, and to avoid controversy. A significant turning point was the 1986 Turkish-Soviet agreement for the supply of Soviet oil and gas to Turkey. Thereafter, Soviet-Turkish trade and business ventures have begun to expand considerably.[17] In late 1989, the large (65,000 tons) Soviet aircraft carrier "Tbilisi" began sea trials, and will eventually use the Bosporus to egress from the Black Sea into the Mediterranean. Here, again, the Turks are highly unlikely to insist on a careful reading of the Montreaux Convention which, by any interpretation, would prohibit the passage of such a capital warship. Simply put, the Turks will ignore the Montreaux Convention unless there were a serious rupture of relations with Moscow.

A European House

There is, then, ample reason to see how Turkey's troubled partnership with NATO has been unfulfilling to Turks. Turks' reasons for being in NATO—to gain political recognition, to enhance economic potential, and (for some Turks) to enter Europe—were distinct from legitimate Turkish concerns about Soviet intentions in 1952 and thereafter. After almost four decades, however, clear and tangible economic or political advantages, with which NATO commitments could be reinforced, are outweighed by a vague but powerful sense that Turkey has been "used" by the West. Such sentiments push Turkey inexorably away from the U.S. and NATO and towards its neighbor north of the Bosporus.

Iraqi aggression in 1990 led to a Turkish acceptance of large U.S. military deployments to Turkey. Whether this crisis will diminish Turkey's sense of exclusion from the West, however, is doubtful; and, there is danger that Ankara's heightened international profile because of the crisis will lead to further resentment if the U.S. and EC, whenever the confrontation with Iraq dissipates, once again appear to shun Turkey.

Today, the Ozal government and most urban elites, want entry into the European Community. Although the Turkish population is divided greatly over the wisdom of Europeanization, other obstacles precluded rapid progress towards such a goal. In December 1989, the 12-nation European Community indefinitely postponed a decision on Turkey's application for full membership, citing "Turkey's near three percent population growth, human rights violations, the unresolved Cyprus question and a comparatively underdeveloped economy."[18]

Some EC members—Denmark, for example—raise historical and contemporary human rights concerns at every stage of considering Turkey's association with the West. Were Turkey to acknowledge the seventy year old massacre of Armenians by Turks, and to make a governmental commitment to end brutality and torture in prisons, West European opinion would be affected positively. Were the Kurds no longer denied outlets for language and cultural expression, the "human rights" issue would also be diminished. Part of the West European concern, too, is in reaction to the late 1970s bloodletting that preceded the last military coup (1980) and a sense that both the killing and the military intervention could happen again if Turkey's fragile democracy is upset through a departure of moderates such as Ozal amid turmoil.[19]

EC unease about Turkey's "civility" is linked to cultural distances between an Islamic nation and the quite different heritage of Western Europe. Certainly, Western Europe has little patience with Islamic fundamentalism. Worries about the rise of such a powerful force in Turkey are often implicit in EC discussion and are emerging as strong right-wing appeals in France and other EC states.[20] Closely related to cultural differences are Western Europe's (and especially Germany's) fear of a further influx of Turks were the open frontiers policy of the EC applied to Turkey as well. With a couple million Turks now in Germany, the prospect of more is discomfiting to many Germans.

The Soviet Union makes no such demands on Turkey. Turks have not only been pushed away from NATO and denied easy entry into the EC; they and the USSR both confront Western Europe and North America's scolding about human rights, and both remain largely excluded from a "European house."

Turkey's sense of exclusion is heightened by the Conventional Forces in Europe (CFE) accord. According to Professor Huseyin Bagci of the Middle East Technical University in Ankara, "With the developments in CFE . . . Turkey will experience a security gap. . . . With the dialogue between the superpowers and the Vienna disarmament talks, the message given to Turkey is clear: 'You just take care of yourself'."[21] As Mikhail Gorbachev and George Bush traded proposals for reduced force levels in these Atlantic-Ural discussions in 1989–1990, the Turkish General Staff and foreign ministry saw the clear potential for an accord to be seriously disadvantageous to their interests. No amount of U.S. assurance (that any accord will have to make military sense for the entire NATO alliance) placates Turkish suspicion. Greek demands to include the Turks' southern (Mediterranean) port of Mersin in CFE angers the Turkish military and public, their counter argument being that the port has nothing to do with European security. By being placed into a "southern zone" of the negotiations, Turks fear that the major cuts soon to be completed in the central region (especially in Germany) are going to enable the Soviets to redeploy more resources into other theatres of military operations (TVD, using the Soviet nomenclature). The Southern TVD (from the Caucasus into Central Asia) would be a plausible beneficiary of relocated assets.

Once again feeling excluded from the core of Europe, Turkish analysts and military planners assess the Soviets as a diminished threat, but with still-ominous capabilities that will not wither due to economically motivated force cutbacks or to reductions imposed by a CFE accord. Were force levels in the Central Region cut to 50% of current NATO levels by CFE, the Turks may see NATO as far less capable of providing aid were aggressive Soviet intentions to recur. And, in Ankara, leaders may well ask if a Germany so intent on an infatuation with Mikhail Gorbachev would ever disrupt budding relations with Moscow to assist (diplomatically or economically, much less militarily) a Turkey threatened with Soviet military intimidation.

Turkish Security in the 1990s

For the moment, there is more that brings Ankara and Moscow together than separates them. Overlapping interests in Southwest Asia have emerged that promote reassessments in Turkey of their longstanding wariness and frequent combat with Russians. Commerce will increase in the 1990s, and strenuous efforts will be made on both sides to avoid wrinkles in a mellowing relationship. To that end, the Soviets may re-double their efforts to achieve a workable compromise concerning ethnic Turks in Bulgaria, while trying to reassure Ankara of its new defensive military doctrine. Turkey will, as with the Mig-29 case and the carrier Tbilisi, bend its NATO role to fit the rapprochement with Moscow.

A past of distrust and warfare will not, however, be forgotten in less than a generation. Episodes such as Charles XII's flight to Turkey after the Battle of Poltava in 1709 or Czar Alexander II's intervention against the Ottomans in the Balkans (1877–78) are, with countless dates and places, deeply embedded in the fabric of both nations' histories. These memories are powerful constraints in the relationship between Turkey and the USSR, and they may be more lasting than a transient symbiosis of regional interests.

Further, Turks have found it difficult, notwithstanding their keen desire to maintain the trend towards warmer ties with Moscow, to ignore Soviet military action in Moslem Azerbaijan. With the Azeris, the Turks share both language and heritage, and bloodshed inflicted by Soviet troops is difficult to accept by the neighboring Turkish population. That Soviet military action in the Caucasus has not been harshly condemned by Ankara must be seen in light of the larger interests of Turkey, and of the careful efforts by the Soviets to ". . . maintai[n] close contact . . ." and appraise the Turks of their intentions.[22]

Yet, the reasons for Turkey's difficulties with NATO and the EC are themselves historical and cultural. In the remainder of this decade, these two strong themes of Turkish history—conflict with Europe and conflict with its principal rival in Southwest Asia—will buffet Turkey's foreign and domestic policies, and challenge as never before its political and military leadership.

Notes

1. For a general account of Islamic influences in Turkish politics, see Ilkay Sunar and Binnaz Tporak, "Islam in Politics: The Case of Turkey," *Government and Opposition* Vol. 18, No. 3 (1983), pp. 421–441.

2. See Jim Bodgener, "Turkish Communists Seek Legality for Their Party," *Financial Times* (June 5, 1990), p. 2.

3. For background on the Presidential selection, see Clyde Haberman's dispatches carried in the *New York Times* in September through November 1989. For example, Haberman's piece, "Turks Seem Heading For New Leadership in Parliament Vote" (October 18, 1989).

4. David Barchard, "Clock May Turn Back to 1970s," *Financial Times* (May 24, 1990).

5. Associated Press dispatch, "Turkish Prime Minster Chosen as President," *The New York Times* (November 1, 1989).

6. Many accounts describe this conflictual history. For the Napoleonic to First World War period, the best book remains Barbara Jelavich's *A Century of Russian Foreign Policy, 1814–1914* (Philadelphia: Lippincott, 1964).

7. See Stephen Engelberg, "Turkey Rebuffs U.S. Plea to Examine Defector's Mig," *New York Times* (March 28, 1989).

8. For assessments of the Turkish contribution to NATO, see NATO Defence Planning Committee, *Enhancing Alliance Collective Security: Shared Roles, Risks*

and Responsibilities in the Alliance (December, 1988), especially pp. 54–55; concerning Turkey's importance for the West if a Gulf crisis occurs, see Albert Wohlstetter, "Die Turkei und die Sicherung der Interessen der NATO," *Europa Archiv*, 16 (1985), pp. 507–514.

9. See "Greek Attacks on Ethnic Turks Alleged," *Financial Times* (January 30, 1990).

10. See Don Oberdorfer, "Angry at Senate Resolution, Turkey Restricts U.S. Forces," *Washington Post* (October 26, 1989).

11. A fuller account of this violence is contained in Chapter 3.

12. Mention of Soviet diplomatic efforts to mediate the Bulgarian-Turkish dispute are found in, for example, Sam Cohen, "Turkey Starts Diplomatic Offensive," *The Christian Science Monitor* (June 28, 1989). Cohen reports that "Turkey . . . asked Soviet leader Mikhail Gorbachev to use his influence on his Warsaw Pact ally. . . . The Soviet ambassador has started a series of contacts in Moscow and Sofia."

13. Author's interviews with faculty and students at the University of Istanbul, February–March, 1989. See also Jim Bodgener, "Ankara Recalls its Envoy From Iran in Islamic Row," *Financial Times* (April 4, 1989) concerning the dispute over the Turkish prohibition of headscarves for women in Turkish higher education institutions.

14. This publication, compiled by American intelligence agencies, appeared under the title *Terrorist Group Profiles* (Washington, D.C.: U.S. Government Printing Office, November, 1988). Although several dozen organizations were mentioned in the Middle East and Western Europe, the PKK was not included.

15. Regarding Iraq's nuclear capabilities (and broadly the proliferation of such capacities), see Leonard Spector, *Nuclear Ambitions* (Boulder, Colo.: Westview Press, 1990).

16. Nazlan Eltan, "To Disarm or Not to Disarm," *Turkish Daily News* (December 18, 1989).

17. This cooperation was solidified in June 1989 with the inauguration of the first commercial Soviet-Turkish joint-venture trading company—"SODE Group A.S."—to market Soviet petrochemicals throughout Turkey, the Middle East and North Africa. Based in Istanbul, the partnership has, as its principal participants, "Sojuzchimexport" in the USSR and Turkiye is Bankasi in Turkey.

18. These issues were noted in Jonathan C. Randal, "The Turkish Identity Crisis," *The International Herald Tribune*. (June 27, 1990). Turkey's ". . . dogged pursuit of full membership in the European Community . . ." has been symbolic of the country's internal conflict over its dual identity. By December 1989, the EC's rejection of Turkey's application for early membership was clear, and the Turks' mix of residual optimism and anger was reported widely. See Clyde Haberman, "Turkey Remains Confident it Will Join European Community," *The New York Times* (March 17, 1990); also, see "That Dispensable Feeling," *The Economist* (May 26, 1990), p. 53. Earlier background regarding Turkish-EC relations is treated by Heinz Kramer, *Die Europaische Gemeinschaft und die Turkei* (Baden-Baden: Nomes Verlas, 1988).

19. This concern is evident in Jim Bodgener, "Lawyer's Murder Revives Extremism Fears in Turkey," *Financial Times* (February 2, 1990).

20. Jean-Marie Le Pen's "National Front" in France, for example, has made Moslem immigration a principal issue, and antagonism towards Turkish entry into the EC has been implicit to his foreign policy stance as well. See Daniel N. Nelson and Julie Baumgarten, "A French Political Crisis," *Christian Science Monitor* (August 31, 1990).

21. Ertan, "To Disarm of Not to Disarm," op. cit.

22. Alan Cowell, "Crackdown is Causing Turks to be Torn by Anger and Desire to Keep Ties," *The New York Times* (January 24, 1990).

6

Athenian Questions

The Political and Economic Quagmire

Constantin Mitsotakis, Greece's new prime minister, survived his first vote of confidence in the Parliament (the 300 member Vouli) on April 26, 1990 using the razor-thin majority he and his New Democracy Party gained in April 8th elections. This early test of Mitsotakis' government, however, was neither the beginning nor the end of a turbulent period in Greek politics.

A socialist government had led Greece through most of the last decade. The decline of PASOK (Panhellenic Socialist Movement) leader Andreas Papandreou had begun in the late 1980s, but was dramatic by early 1989. As prime minister from 1981 to 1989, Papandreou's power waned when allegations surfaced that he either urged George Koskotas, a banker who then fled to the United States, to embezzle over $200 million from the Bank of Crete for PASOK coffers *or* he accepted bribes to allow such activities to take place. Notwithstanding Papandreou's vigorous denials, the scandal, and revelations that he had ordered illegal phone taps against political opponents, contributed to a precipitous decline in his personal popularity.[1]

Also, his personal life was highly scrutinized when the seventy-two-year-old prime minister publicly courted a former Greek airlines flight attendant, Dimitra Liani, who is in her mid-30s. That Papandreou finally divorced his American wife to marry Dimitra improved public assessments of the affair very little. Although Papandreou's supporters rallied in early 1990, the genesis of PASOK's ouster from government in 1989, and the eventual emergence of a conservative government a year later, were the financial and personal scandals around the prime minister.[2]

Elections were called for June 18, 1989, when a strange right-left alliance was formed between New Democracy with 145 deputies at that time and the 28 Communist Party (the KKE in its Greek initials) deputies against PASOK. Their sole purpose was to prosecute those high ranking Socialists involved in the scandal. Parliament later ordered Papandreou

110   *Athenian Questions*

and five of his ministers to stand trial. Were this trial to occur, both the proceedings and results would engender a political circus in Athens.

The first 1989 coalition lasted only until November of that year when a second coalition of all three major parties was sworn in. Appointed then as prime minister was Xenophon Zolotas, 85, former governor of the Bank of Greece. Zolotas was intended as a non-party leader whose goal was to maintain order and to act as caretaker while the nation prepared for the April 1990 elections.[3] Cabinet posts were distributed among the parties according to the percentage received in the previous elections. Because there was no consensus among the parties, the Zolotas cabinet was unable to institute any new policies, and economic problems accumulated.

The worsening economy aided Mitsotakis. As a former finance minister, his campaign stressed the need for single-minded leadership to lower inflation, cut deficits, curb unemployment, and prepare the country for integration into the EC. Even many PASOK supporters acknowledged the dangerous direction of governmental spending, foreign debt and inflation. By late 1989, the nation faced 15% inflation—the highest in Europe. Further, an already large trade deficit was threatening to increase by yet another 10%. Under Papandreou, the government had painted itself into a corner by expanding greatly the publicly-owned sector of the economy which, by 1989, was losing money and woefully inefficient. Consequently, the Greek treasury was spending billions of dollars to support dozens of failing corporations, adding greatly to annual deficits (the 1989 deficit was half again higher than 1988), and accumulating public debt to a level of 39% of GNP. Subsidizing non-competitive industry, by one estimate, cost the Greek economy the equivalent of $40,000 for each job in those corporations.[4]

Other social concerns such as a rampant spread of illegal drugs have also risen quickly as political issues, and Mitsotakis played on this theme as well during his spring 1990 campaign. The public was responsive to the New Democracy Party's charges against PASOK that, by their example or by their inefficiency, they had "allowed" Greek organized crime and drug trafficking to rise while failing to protect traditional values. Although many economic and international issues were interwoven with Greeks' social concerns, the latter were particularly helpful to Mitsotakis among older voters and women in the electorate.[5]

Mitsotakis' victory, in which he secured 46.9% of the vote, rested precariously on gains in Athens and Piraeus.[6] Further, although he did win 150 seats in the Vouli, he had to obtain the vital support of one other non-New Democracy deputy for a parliamentary majority. The individual who swung over to back Mitsotakis was Costas Stefanopoulos,

Athenian Questions

the only deputy elected from the right of center Democratic Renewal Party.[7]

Mitsotakis could not claim a clear mandate for several reasons. First, a new electoral system instituted a year ago by Papandreou, while he still held a parliamentary majority, allocates seats in the Vouli on the basis of strict proportionality. Rather than being able to win in each district by simply receiving a plurality, potentially creating a parliamentary majority for a party that had far less than 50% of all votes, but was the biggest vote getter in most districts, the new system requires that a party receive almost half (47%) of the ballots to claim half of the Vouli seats. Parliamentary majorities are thus more difficult to achieve, and the parliamentary vote less determined by regional or class-based strengths of parties.

Second, Greeks were unwilling to depart entirely from their support of Papandreou, regardless of scandals, because he was perceived as the victim of bullying by the other major parties. The PASOK leader regained ground in public opinion polls in the first months of 1990 ". . . because of the appearance of vindictiveness in the prosecution of him and others."[8] This underdog image was, of course, cultivated by Papandreou, although the precise effect is unknown.

More certain, however, is the inability of Mitsotakis to use the scandal issue to its full potential. By participating in the temporary coalition government from June 1989 through early 1990 that involved cooperation with Papandreou, Mitsotakis was less able to "pin" the corruption issue on the PASOK leader. Although Mitsotakis' candidacy was given initial momentum by personal and financial clouds around the former prime minister, the New Democracy leader sensed a reservoir of public sympathy for Papandreou and thus concentrated on the need for ". . . a strong majority to lead the country out of its economic morass" in campaigning.[9]

Third, some Greek journalists suggested that their countrymen "are more afraid of Thatcherism than Communism."[10] The unraveling of social welfare, the enlargement of already significant social inequalities, and rising unemployment are fears that are not confined to the Greek lower classes. Public opinion data do, indeed, suggest a profound reluctance to abolish government subsidies and welfare programs initiated since 1974. Mitsotakis was thus chary about proposing a radical shift towards the private sector, and instead spoke often during the campaign of protecting people's incomes and creating jobs without dwelling on the many hurtful elements of the austerity he knew he would have to impose.[11] Greek Socialists spoke bitterly of Mitsotakis' deceitful campaigning, arguing that the New Democracy Party would impose austerity in a way oblivious to the harm caused to the working class.[12]

The economic policies of the previous administrations have left Greece, as one senior finance ministry official is reputed to have said, with "one foot in Europe and one foot in the third world." In order for Greece to prepare itself for 1992, the leaders of the new government immediately began to institute an austere economic reform program, the most drastic in Europe outside of the East. The day after receiving its mandatory vote of confidence, Economics Minister George Souflias announced sharp tax and price increases, without compensatory wage hikes. Increasing state income while curbing consumption are to be two sides of Mitsotakis policy, and these first steps were to enhance income. Particularly hard hit are taxes applied to alcohol, gasoline and tobacco. The government is also going to slash spending in arenas of other public services.[13]

These first steps mirror drastic policies urged by the Organization for Economic Cooperation and Development in an early 1990 report on the Greek economy. With the inflation rate as of early 1990 climbing to almost 18%, three times the EC average, trade running a large deficit, and foreign debt likely to hit $3 billion in 1990 alone, changes in the economy must be across the board. To salvage the Greek economy there must be simultaneous action to heighten taxation, raise industrial standards, liberalize capital movement and limit governmental subsidies to industries. This broad, all-encompassing effort would necessitate efforts even beyond those thus far imposed by Mitsotakis. There is no single problem, but a complex intermingling of economic difficulties. Debates about where Greece's economic quagmire began—in 1970s growth based on foreign borrowing not exports, or in 1980s emphasis on state-owned, unproductive enterprises and social welfare, or externally, in the world market and Greece's peripheral role in it—may be moot. The country must now try to do everything at once or face worsening conditions, and a slide back from development and prosperity.[14]

George Souflias, Mitsotakis' first minister of national economy, created a multi-pronged plan to revitalize the Greek economy. Privatization, first in twenty-eight industries that suffer from high debt levels, has the ultimate goal of selling off all enterprises except those in defense manufacturing.[15] Simultaneously, the new governor of the Central Bank of Greece, Dimitri Halikias, has sought to strengthen monetary policy, while recognizing that the country's problems are structural—a need to gear production to the "pattern of domestic and foreign demand."[16] The overall plan requires, as well, thorough tax reform to enhance incentives for investments and productivity, to make the tax system compatible with the EC, and to broaden the tax base while closing loopholes. These ambitious goals, according to Finance Minister Yannis Palaiokrassas, must be linked to a severe reduction in government expenditures.[17]

The European Community's council of ministers is expected to "pass judgment" periodically on the Greek efforts to reform its economy. EC membership is generally supported among Greeks, and compliance with austerity may be accepted by many.

But the General Confederation of Greek Workers, with a membership encompassing 33% of the work force, demanded a 23% boost in wages as soon as the new Mitsotakis government was installed. The reaction of organized labor to the New Democracy economic program was quick and angry, and strongly suggests that Greeks will experience continued labor unrest in the early 1990s. Greek labor had not, of course, been accumstomed to suffering from austerity; during the Zolotas caretaker administration, as deficits mounted, the threat of strikes had brought swift concessions from the government and wage increases well above those indexed to inflation.[18]

By September 1990, strikes by bank employees, trash collectors and public service workers were followed by several mid-week 48-hour general strikes. The general strikes by over a million workers were mounted as the General Confederation and two smaller labor federations sought to derail Mitsotakis' austerity measures. Workers were particularly aggrieved by the conservative government's plans to reduce pensions and raise the age at which government employees can retire, both of which were steps designed to cut back parts of PASOK social welfare while reducing deficits.[19] Although the workers may lose some of their costly privileges, compromises will be forced on Mitsotakis as well. Ongoing conflict between the New Democracy administration and labor may aid PASOK and the extreme left, and are sure to slow the Greek economic recovery.

Greek Foreign Policy Adjustments

Since the Greek Civil War in the late 1940s, Greek-American security ties have been close yet troubled. The Truman Doctrine was an American response to many stimuli, and represented a U.S. decision to assume global burdens in the face of perceived challenges to Western interests. Yet the threat of a communist victory in the Greek Civil War was a proximate "cause" of President Truman's March, 1947 pronouncement guaranteeing aid to "all free peoples who are resisting attempted subjugation by armed minorities or outside pressure."

As close as the ties have been, however, the relationship has been strewn with obstacles. Persistent Greek-Turkish tension often left the United States trying to keep both sides quiescent. The Greek military junta (1967–1974) also created resentment of the U.S.—particularly during the Nixon Administration—for what seemed to be tacit support for "the colonels."[20] Perhaps most troublesome from Washington's standpoint was the radical rhetoric of Andreas Papandreou during the 1980s who often and loudly made statements critical of the U.S. and its foreign policy.

Greek-American relations during the Papandreou era were characterized by a mixture of rhetoric and defiance against the western alliance. While publicly declaring that his government would withdraw Greece from NATO and remove the U.S. military presence, Papandreou's actual stance was more incremental. Under Papandreou, Greece refused to participate in certain NATO exercises taking place in the Aegean Sea, opposed cruise and Pershing II missile deployments in the early 1980s, and often lectured about American efforts to impose a subservient status on Greece. Nevertheless, official membership in both political and military arms of the alliance was renewed and maintained under Papandreou. And, despite the prime minister's open calls for an end to U.S. bases in Greece, Papandreou understood the importance of such military assistance.[21] Greeks view the seven to ten ratio of aid to Greece and Turkey as vital to maintaining stability and a balance of power in the region.[22] Papandreou was thus caught in a conundrum; while he wished to remove the American presence in Greece, he could not deny the importance of that presence in protecting his nation's security.

Negotiations on renewing arrangements for U.S. bases in Greece, that had originated in a 1952 accord after the end of the Civil War, were protracted and difficult. Papandreou had long said that the Hellinikon air base should be evacuated by Americans, and his rhetoric coincided with terrorist attacks against U.S. military personnel in Greece.

Finally, because of budgetary constraints, changing strategic needs, and impatience with Greek demands, the United States made a unilateral decision in 1990 to close the bases of Hellinikon (which is adjacent to the Athens international airport, just outside the city) and Nea Makri (near Attica).[23]

This decision once again strained relations between the United States and Greece. Although the Papandreou leadership advocated publicly a withdrawal of American forces, a seventeen month extension of the leases had been granted by the interim coalition government. The Greeks were unprepared for the January 1990 American announcement, particularly because of Greece's impending election only a few months later.

Shortly after the announcement of the closings (the Pentagon wants to maintain two other bases on Crete, especially the huge naval facility at Souda Bay), concern arose in Athens about the economic effects of the closings and the future balance of power in the Aegean between Greece and Turkey.[24] Reduction of U.S. troops has been coupled with talk of cuts in military aid from the United States—talk heightened by Senator Dole's proposal to reallocate U.S. foreign aid to benefit Eastern

Europe. Dole's proposal may have represented an effort by the Bush Administration to test the waters for cutting aid to Greece, Israel, Egypt, the Philippines, Turkey and Pakistan in order to facilitate the United States commitment to the fledgling democracies in Eastern Europe. Greece was criticized by Dole for not cashing $818 million in military credits, implying that it was being intended for other uses than buying arms from the United States.

While military aid to Turkey would also be reduced under this proposal, Greece is anxious to see that those cuts match their own and that the balance of power in the Aegean is maintained. Anything that might end U.S. adherence to the seven to ten ratio of American aid to Greece and Turkey, respectively, would upset a fundamental tenet of Greek defense policy.[25] And, with the closing of two of the four American bases, the Greeks immediately began to wonder whether or not the $350 million in U.S. military aid received annually in lieu of rent for the bases would be reduced substantially.[26]

Another point of conflict between Greece and the United States during the 1980s was the PASOK policy towards the Middle East. Greece joined Italy and Spain in criticizing the U.S. action against Libya in 1986, and resisted extradition of a Palestinian terrorist, Mohammed Rashid, sought by American authorities for alleged involvement in the 1982 bombing of a Pan Am passenger plane. Papandreou and his PASOK party had been attempting to build a bridge between the West and the Arab World and believed the U.S. action threatened their chances at becoming effective mediators. They held the view that the American aggression might create a violent backlash against the West by Islamic fundamentalists.

Fear of Turkey has already affected Greece's participation in talks between NATO and the Warsaw Pact on the reduction of conventional forces in Europe, i.e., CFE. The issue is over the southern Turkish Mediterranean port of Mersin. The Greeks raised this issue vehemently just before CFE talks were to begin in early 1989 and, although set aside at that time, may again become an obstacle. Athens wants the port to be subject to treaty requirements because it is used as a supply center for the Turkish military on Cyprus. The Turkish response is that the port should be exempt from CFE because of its importance in defense of Turkey from the Middle East. Few countries in the rest of NATO find Mersin to be an issue worth damaging Atlantic-Urals arms control, but to the Greeks such concerns rise to significant heights.[27]

Amid emerging doubts about a continued security relationship with the United States, and foreseeing a future without superpower guarantees in the Aegean, Greece has begun to take unilateral and bilateral steps to enhance its security. It was revealed, for instance, that Greece has fortified the Aegean islands of Lesbos, Chios, Samos, Kos and Icaria with tanks, self-propelled artillery and other heavy weapons. This would be an apparent violation of the 1947 Paris Treaty, as well as the 1923 Lausanne Treaty.[28] In addition, Athens has sought security links with Bulgaria—signing one protocol in late 1986, and expanding contacts in 1989 (These matters are discussed more fully in both the chapters concerning Bulgaria and Turkey).[29]

Clearly directed against Turkey, these forces in the Aegean and contact with Bulgaria exhibits the Greeks' questioning of where they will be in ten years. Close relations with Sofia not only help vis-à-vis the Turks, of course, but also limit the potential for Macedonia to be used as an issue against Greece by more than one of its northern neighbors. Yugoslavia recently re-opened the "Macedonian Issue" when it claimed that the Macedonian minority in northern Greece was being mistreated. The Greek government contends that no such minority exists, maintaining its stance that all Greeks of Slavic origin migrated to Yugoslavia after World War II.

Summary

Mitsotakis' unstable majority, significant economic difficulties and disturbing international signs all cloud Athens' immediate political future. Greece is a country not yet in a dangerous crisis. But Greeks unquestionably have reason for apprehension.

The Mitsotakis government has charted a course for economic recovery fraught with numerous obstacles, most obviously labor unrest as the austere budgets and privatization lead to higher unemployment and lower living standards. Externally, the government must also repair relations with the West, while building new security arrangements perhaps in lieu of a longstanding American presence in the Aegean separating Greece and Turkey.

During this period of intense transition, questions about Greece's future abound, although the promise of both enhanced prosperity and an improved international position warrant some confidence. But few people in Athens expect the early 1990s to be a tranquil period.

Notes

1. For details on the issues focused on Papandreou that had emerged by June 1989 when PASOK was ousted see, Carol Reed, "Greek Premier Faces Electoral Test," *Christian Science Monitor* (June 16, 1989), p. 6.

2. Comments on this political environment and the damage caused to Papandreou receive comment in Valerie M. Hudson and John C. Thomas, "Pandora's Ballot Box," *Christian Science Monitor* (June 15, 1989).

Athenian Questions

3. An account of this coalition, and expectations regarding Zolotas, was offered by Paul Anastasi, "Greeks Agree On a Broad Coalition Until April," *The New York Times* (November 22, 1989).

4. Assessments of the Greek economic condition were ominous by the end of 1989. See Howard La Franchi, "High Debt, Inflation Signal Austerity Program," *Christian Science Monitor* (November 22, 1989) and in the same edition of the *Monitor* an unattributed report on "European Community Nudges Athens Toward Making Reforms." An OECD evaluation was highly critical in early 1990. See Tim Carrington, "Greek Economy Needs Overhaul, OECD Declares," *The Wall Street Journal* (February 1, 1990), p. A6.

5. The importance of these social issues was stressed to me during April 1990 discussions in Athens with leaders of both PASOK and New Democracy.

6. See "Greek Conservatives Within One Seat of Majority," *International Herald Tribune* (April 9, 1990). p. 1; also reporting on this narrow victory was *The Economist* (April 14, 1990), p. 46.

7. "The Importance of Being Costas," *The Economist* (April 14, 1990), p. 46.

8. Panayotis Dimitras, a Greek pollster and political commentator on Athens television, as quoted by Alan Cowell, "Fringe Groups Swaying Athens Vote," *The New York Times* (April 8, 1990).

9. Edward Cody, "Greek Conservative Within 1 Seat of Majority," *Washington Post* (April 10, 1990), p. A1.

10. Nikos Dimou, political commentator for Athenian newspapers and television, as quoted by Cowell, op. cit.

11. The Greek fear of Thatcherism is a quote from Nikos Dimou as cited by Cowell, op. cit. Mitsotakis' campaign positions on the economy were reported in "The Importance of Being Costas," *The Economist*, op. cit., p. 46–47.

12. These assessments were made during conversations with former members of the PASOK government in Athens (April 1990).

13. Kerin Hope, "Mitsotakis Faces Hard Decisions on Economy," *Financial Times* (April 10, 1990).

14. For a summary of the OECD report, see Tim Carrington, "Greek Economy Needs Overhaul, OECD Declares," *The Wall Street Journal* (February 1, 1990), p. A6.

15. Kerin Hope, "Greece Offers 28 Companies to Private Sector," *Financial Times* (May 21, 1990).

16. "Monetary Policy as a Bulwark to Inflation," Interview with the governor of the Central Bank of Greece, Dimitri Halikias, *Washington Post* (September 24, 1990).

17. "Tax Reform in Greece," Interview with Minister of Finance Yannis Palaiokrassas, *Washington Post* (September 24, 1990).

18. Kerin Hope, "Greeks Win Extra Wage Increases," *Financial Times* (February 21, 1990), p. 3.

19. Reports on these strikes included, "Greece Brought to a Standstill by Strikes Against Austerity," *The New York Times* (September 21, 1990) and Kerin Hope, "Greek Workers Stage Third Strike Over Pension Scheme," *Financial Times* (September 26, 1990).

20. This point is made, for example, in F. Stephen Larrabee, "The Southern Periphery: Greece and Turkey," in Paul Shoup, ed. *Problems of Balkan Security* (Washington, D.C.: The Wilson Center Press, 1990), p. 178–179.

21. A complete consideration of Greek foreign and defense policy during the Karamanlis and Papandreou periods (1974–1989) is Thanos Veremis, "Greece and Nato: Continuity and change," in John Chipman, ed., *NATO's Southern Allies* (London: Routledge, 1988), pp. 236–286. Veremis' summary judgment about Papandreous' underlying realism is suggested especially on p. 278.

22. An example of how vital this balance is to Greece, and the role of the 7:10 ratio in assuring it, is Kyra Adams' article, "New Picture in Relations with the United States," *Kiriakatiki Elevtherotipia* (January 28, 1990), p. 8, as translated in FBIS-WEU 90-Occ-S (February 16, 1990), p. 92.

23. Kerin Hope, "US To Close Two of Four Military Bases in Greece," *Financial Times* (January 29, 1990).

24. Comments on the economic consequences were numerous. One instance is the editorial commentary in *To Vima Tis Kiriakis* (January 28, 1990), p. 11. Regarding the larger security implications see, for example, "Effects of the Closings," *To Vima Tis Kiziakis* (January 28, 1990), pp. 10–11., Both articles are translated in FBIS-WEU-90-033-S (February 16, 1990), p. 93.

25. The core tenets of Greek defense policy, and the critical maintenance of an Aegean balance via the 7:10 ratio, are detailed in Thanos Veremis, *Greece and NATO: Continuity and Change* (London: Routledge, 1988).

26. More detailed information on the level of U.S. foreign military sales credits provided to Greece are contained in "Greece and Turkey: U.S. Foreign Assistance Facts," *Issue Brief* (Washington, D.C.: Congressional Research Service, November 25, 1988).

27. R. Jeffrey Smith, "Dispute Between Turkey, Greece Delaying Action on Treaty," *Washington Post* (November 23, 1989).

28. Douglas Barrie, "Aegean Forces Detailed," *Janes Defence Weekly* (April 14, 1990), pp. 680–681.

29. See also Paul Anastasi, "Athens Joins Sofia to Curb Ethnic Strife," *The New York Times* (February 10, 1990).

Conclusion: Balkan Pasts, Balkan Futures

Europe's twentieth century began with rumblings in its eastern half—portents of a terrible decade from the onset of the Balkan Wars (1912) until the end of the Russian Civil War. Between these years, the Balkans erupted with revolts against the Ottoman Turks and Russian intervention, which were then followed by the conflagration of World War I triggered by a royal assassination in Bosnia, but fought throughout the Baltic to Bosporus corridor.

Allied victory in 1918 ended fighting in the West of Europe, but Russians and other peoples within the old Czarist empire, Poles, Hungarians, and all of the Balkans continued to battle. In Southeastern Europe, the demise of both the Austro-Hungarian Empire and the Ottoman Empire were catalysts for years more of bloodshed and political turmoil. The Romanians fought the Hungarian forces of Bela Kun in 1919, the Greeks invaded Asia Minor and were thrown back by Ataturk in 1922 after several years of intermittent post-Versailles warfare, and other battles, coups, and assassinations occurred with frequency.

If there was calm between the world wars in the Balkans, it seems to have been imposed by military or civilian authoritarians, anti-democratic monarchs, or unsure party coalitions. In the Balkans, particularly, this was not a time in which steady political advances were made. Instead, weak states and leadership uncertainty prevailed in Southeastern Europe, with governments able to address few of the critical problems inherited from the region's domination by declining empires.

That there were great Balkan leaders between the First and Second World Wars cannot be denied. For different reasons, and because of distinct personal attributes, the likes of Ioan Bratianu and Nicolae Titulescu in Romania, Stamboliski in Bulgaria, Venizelos in Greece and (of course) Mustafa Kemal Ataturk in Turkey *all* rose above many others and offered the hope of stability and development in the region, albeit not necessarily

119

120   *Conclusion*

democracy. And there *were* transient international successes constructed by pragmatic and far-reaching diplomacy . . . a Little Entente formed in 1920–1921, a Balkan Entente in 1934, and Greek-Turkish reconciliation in the mid-1920s.

But democratic progress was elusive. Although it is an oversimplification, one is tempted to note a political uniformity in the region—". . . an almost identical evolution . . . for all the Balkan states"[1]—during the inter-war period, that provided little experience or trust on which to base post–World War II resistance to communist party rule. Plagued by socioeconomic and ethnonationalist schisms, and threatened by neighboring states with irredentist claims, the Balkan states had little success with competitive elections, the rule of law, and other critical components of democracy. Royal dictatorships of Romania's Carol II and Boris in Bulgaria, both relying on the military for ultimate control, wiped away any chance for parliamentary government. Greece's shaky political system, after the disastrous military campaign in Asia Minor, went through army coups and counter-coups, eventually reaching the dictatorship of General Metaxas (1936–1941) under the nominal monarchy of George II. King Zog in Albania ruled in a similarly authoritarian fashion, although his own autonomy was more and more constrained by Mussolini. Turkey relied on its national hero, Ataturk, until his death in 1938, but that very reliance precluded anything other than a personalistic system; even after his death, Ataturk's memory was a strand of legitimacy for subsequent governments.

The Balkans reached World War II without any parliamentary democracies in the region. Although the degree of repression by secret police and the extent of militarism in governments varied, the capacities with which to resist a renewal of authoritarianism, albeit under a different banner, were woefully inadequate. From legislative and administrative skills, to the notions of individual liberties and open societies, Balkan countries were denied any reservoir from which to draw in the second half of the century.

Since World War II, we have seen enormous socioeconomic and political progress in much of Europe; the economic development of Mediterranean Europe, especially of Spain and Italy, has been impressive, while economic recovery and democractic experiences in Western Germany and Italy have pushed back the memories of fascism and socialized two generations of citizens regarding plural societies and the rule of law. With global restructuring now underway as post-war bipolarity ends, such a two-generation "cushion" between defeat in World War II and the demise of superpower dominance in Europe gives us reason to be confident about the survival of democracy in Central Europe. The end of dictatorships in Spain and Portugal, and the resolution of constitutional

Conclusion

uncertainties in France also speak to Western Europe's domestic advances. The European Community, of course, is the premier accomplishment, carrying with it the potential for a fundamental reorientation of citizenship and the role of states.

But Balkan peoples have not benefited from such changes. The rigidity of communist rule, and the damage generated by central planning and total state ownership are nowhere more evident than in Bulgaria, Romania, and Albania. The inadequacy of halfway measures to reform communist systems is nowhere more palpable than in Yugoslavia. Turkey's condition suggests strongly the dichotomies of secularism and fundamentalism, urban and rural, European and Middle East, civilian and military, and the danger that these twains will never meet. And, in Greece, having endured a military dictatorship and a loudly proclaimed socialism, governments have limited mandates and fragile capacities with which to deal with mounting socioeconomic issues.

In the twentieth century, the states and peoples of the Balkans have been excluded from much of Europe's progress, both before and after World War II. We can "blame" imperialism and communism, perhaps, for the punishments absorbed by Southeastern Europe. Yet, the root cause arguably lies in the weakness of indigenous political structures in a region wherein other identities and loyalties have paramount importance.

Balkan Futures

Based only on indications drawn from political behaviors and socioeconomic conditions circa 1990, there are few bright spots for Balkan prognoses. But this summary judgment, were it left unqualified, would overlook historical undercurrents and cross-national characteristics that warrant more optimism.

Southeastern Europe need no longer be cut off from the rest of Europe and the continent's socioeconomic and political advances. The entry of Greece into the EC, and the longstanding desire of the Turkish government to join as well, is part of the Balkans' "rejoining" of Europe. Postcommunist systems are jettisoning aspects of previous government's economic policies that made them incompatible with Western Europe, and trying to entice Western investments while accepting advice and assistance about "marketizing" their economies. Age-old divisions between Eastern and Western Europe may, propelled both by political realities (the end of superpower hegemony and cold war confrontation in Central Europe) and the diffusion of values and interests via telecommunications, help to enhance the political development of the region and accelerate its economic recovery.

122   *Conclusion*

These new interests may be coupled with resurgent "old" interests in the Balkans. The region's role as a "buffer" vis-à-vis Islamic fundamentalism and/or radical Arab nationalism is seen by some Western and Central Europeans as one of increasing importance—due both to demographic issues as well as the militancy of a segment of Islam. Further, West European powers will retain their interest in avoiding anyone's dominance of the Balkans, which would mean an implicit challenge for control of the Bosporus, Eastern Mediterranean and adjacent seas. For more than a century, Russia was the country against which British and French concern was directed. Now joined by the EC membership as a whole, however, the interest will be to ensure a balance in the region, and to avoid an inviting vacuum into which forces hostile to European security might be tempted.

The United States, since the Wilsonian principles contributed to the birth of Yugoslavia, and particularly since post-war support for Tito and Greece embedded American interests in the Balkans, will be a party to this condominium of external powers desirous of Balkan stability. There may be differences between the United States and European states in their assessments of Balkan issues and needs, but all will agree that no other power should once again assert hegemony over Southeastern Europe.

Yet, from within each Balkan country, there is also a new-found potential that existed minimally in prior decades. When the region fought to rid itself of Ottoman and Hapsburg suzerainty, there were examples of nationalism and the appearance of notable statesmen and military figures. By and large, however, political life remained a play in which only rulers, landowners and the church had leading roles. Peasants were acted "upon," in a political culture that never invoked a participatory ethos.

That has now changed irrevocably. Whereas Stephen Fischer-Galati could speak accurately of Eastern Europe's political retardation in terms of autocracy, orthodoxy and nationality,[2] the end of the twentieth century finds these characteristics breaking down. By the last decades of the century, new groups of political actors have emerged forcefully in the eastern half of Europe—workers, the intelligentsia, professional strata— with interests such as ecology, peace and justice, etc. that create many cross-cutting cleavages. These groups and individuals have become *participants,* sometimes incrementally, but always courageously. Popular determination *not* to return to dictatorships, enthusiasm *for* public activism, and impatience with false responsiveness of government are all evident. There is an unmistakable willingness, as there has not been before in the Balkans, to reject makeshift changes, smokescreens and shell games with which they have been all too familiar. Scandal has knocked Papandreou out of office in Greece, while the Motherland Party of Ozal lost its

Conclusion 123

mandate in Turkey due to its incremental approach to change and to a series of scandals. In Bulgaria, President Mladenov is forced to resign, while Romanians opposed to President Iliescu and the Front refuse to end protests and strikes and Albanians swarm to foreign embassy compounds to demand, via mass flight, systemic change.

Mass politics and public legitimation have dawned on the Balkans. Turning the corner away from a rigidly defined political sphere in which aristocrats or party elites were all that mattered is enormously difficult and fraught with great uncertainty. Yet, this is a strength from below that was often absent in these corner of Europe; peasants toiled, and their labor formed the building blocks of the economy and army, but there was never any participatory involvement. Now, however, leaders and their policies are matters of public discourse, and it would be impossible to once again diminish the latitude of public political life.

These are not insignificant strengths. A diminishing division between parts and regions of Europe will rejoin the Balkans' socioeconomic and political future increasingly with the rest of the continent. The emergence of participatory political cultures expands the "resource base" of Balkan political systems beyond the narrow aristocratic or ideological elite stratum. This broadening and deepening, one might say, of Balkan politics may together be long-term sources of the region's regeneration.

For the 1990s, however, the obstacles to Balkan stability and prosperity that have been enumerated in this volume are substantial and immediate. The intensity of present discontents in Yugoslavia, Romania, Albania and Bulgaria, and difficult economic austerity and social issues confronting Greek and Turkish democracies, will all present challenges to the capacities of these political systems. If these hurdles for the 1990s can be managed, then the emerging sources of strength—links to all of Europe and indigenous participatory cultures—will enhance the prospects for regional development in the coming century.

Notes

1. Sherman D. Spector and Rene Ristelheuber, *A History of the Balkan Peoples* (New York: Twayne Publishers, 1971), p. 305.

2. See Stephen Fischer-Galati, "Introduction," in Stephen Fischer-Galati, *Man, State and Society in East European History* (New York: Praeger, 1970), pp. v–ix.

Index

Abbas, Abdul, 50
Abdic, Fikret, 42
"Achille Lauro" highjacking, 51
Adevarul, 85
  See also Frontul Salvarii Nationale
Aegean Sea, 98, 100
  maritime incidents, 98
Agrarian Party. *See* Bulgaria
"Agrogate." *See* Agrokomerc
Agroindustrial centers
  in Romania, 12
Agrokomerc, 42, 43
Albania
  Albanian separatism, 20, 49
  birth rate, 43
  and China, 21, 22
  Christians, 43
  and communist rule, 121
  departure from Warsaw Pact, 21, 24
  domestic and foreign policy, 20–23
  economic activity, 123
  and Greece, 22, 26
  Macedonian minority, 35
  mass flight, 123
  Moslems, 43
  and NATO, 21, 22
  and NSWP states, 22
  population growth in, 3
  threat of Soviet or NSWP invasion, 26
  trade with East Germany, 22
  and Turkey, 22
  and the USSR, 20–24, 28, 34(n66)
  and Warsaw Pact, 20, 21, 23
  and Western Europe, 22
  and Yugoslavia, 21, 20, 23, 26, 28, 43, 44
  See also Croatia, Croatian crisis; Hoxha, Enver; Kosovo; Serbian nationalism
Alexander II, 2, 105

Alia, Ramiz, 4, 22
Anev, Tsviatko, 14
Ankara, 91, 100
Ankara Treaty (1953), 17
Anti-Nazi partisans
  in the BPA, 14
Arab-Israeli conflict, 51
Archduke Ferdinand, 2
Atanosov, Georgi, 63
  and ethnic Turks, 58
Ataturk, Mustafa Kemal, 91, 95, 119, 120
Atlantic-Ural (CFE) discussions, 104
Austria, 16
Austro-Hungarian Empire, 35, 119
  and the Balkans, 1, 2
  and Croatia, 1
Azerbaijan, 101, 105
  Moslems in, 101
  See also Union of Soviet Socialist Republics, Islamic fundamentalism

Bacanu, Petre Mihai, 79
Bagci, Huseyin, 103
Balkan Pact (1934), 17
  disintegration, 18
Balkan Pact (1954), 17
Balkans
  All-Balkan conference in Athens (1976), 19
  Balkan entente, 120
  "Balkan imbroglio," vii
  Balkan union, 17, 21
  Balkan wars, 119
  defined, 1
  and Europe, 121
  foreign ministers conference (1988), 15, 22, 33(n51)
  and marketization, 121
  and the Ottoman Turks, 2
  poverty in, 3

125

and telecommunications, 121
and the USSR, 2, 26, 28
warfare in, 2
and the Warsaw Pact, 28
and Western Europe, 20, 121, 122
World War II, 120
See also Balkan Pact
Bank
of Crete, 109
of Greece, 110
Battle of Poltava, 105
BCP. *See* Bulgarian Communist Party
Belgrade
Balkan meeting (1988), 22
protest in, 41
Belgrade Declaration (1955), 17
Bender, Peter, 27
Beron, Peter, 63
Bessarabia, 30(n6)
Black Sea, 95, 102
Bobu, Emil, 75
Borba, 47
Bosnia, 119
and the JNA, 46
Bosnia-Hercogovina, 5, 42
Bosnian Party Central Committee, 42
Bosporus, 102, 119
Soviet interest in, 24
Botez, Sorin, 76
BPA. *See* Bulgarian People's Army
Bratianu, Ioan, 119
Brezhnev, Leonid
and Romania, 9
warnings to Ceausescu, 29(n3)
See also Brezhnev Doctrine
Brezhnev Doctrine, 9, 21, 33(n54)
and Bulgaria, 56
Brovet, Stane, 39
Brown, James, 21
BSP. *See* Bulgarian Socialist Party
Bucharest, 84
August 1968 rally in, 9
rallies in, 10
Bukovina, 30(n6)
Bulgaria
Agrarian Party, 56
agriculture, 60
"Chavdar" Partisans, 68
civilian airline, 13

"Club for the Support of Perestroika and Glasnost." *See* Discussion Club
and the CMEA, 12
and communist rule, 121
Council of Ministers, 67
coup attempt planned (1965), 14
debt, 61
democracy in, 55. *See also* election monitoring in
Democratic League for the Defense of Human Rights, 57
demonstrations, strikes, 57, 59
Discussion Club for the Support of Glasnost and Perestroika, 58, 62
domestic and foreign policy in, 12–16
Eco-Glasnost in, 58, 59, 62, 63
economic austerity, 123
economic reform, 56, 59, 61
economy, 60, 61
election monitoring in, 64
elections in June, 1990, 5, 55
Electoral Commission, 65
and Greece, 28
Islam in, 56
living standards in, 12
and Macedonia, 2, 19. *See also* Greek-Bulgarian accord
media. *See Narodna Armiya; Ostechestven Front; Podkrepa*
military, 23, loyalty of, 55
military expenditures, 12, 31(n20)
Ministry of Internal Affairs, 68
Muslims in, 3, 14, 57, 60, 62, 99
National Agrarian Union, 66, 70
National Assembly, 64; commission on ethnic hostilities, 63
New Economic Mechanism (NEM), 60, 61
and NSWP, 9, 13
Orthodox Christianity in, 3
and Ottoman empire, 2
parliament in, 56
Prokurator, 62
rail capacity, 13
Red Army control, 97
Romanian elections, 26
secret police, 63, 99
"Sixth Department," 68
Stalinist elements, 56
Supreme court, 62

Index

127

and Thrace, 2
trade, 13, 15. *See also* Bulgaria, and
the CMEA
and Turkey, 15, 28, 69, 99, 100
Turkish minority, 56–60, 62, 99,
100, 102, 104, 106
and the USSR, 12–14, 27, 28, 56
and the Warsaw Pact, 8, 13, 15, 16,
25, 55, 66
and Yugoslavia, 27, 51
See also Turkey, Nationals in
Bulgaria; Zhivkov, Todor
Bulgarian army
and the BPA, 14
and domestic unrest, 59
and economy, 61
and ethnic disputes, 59
and Soviet dominance, 13
Bulgarian Communist Party (BCP), 5,
62, 67, 99
central committee, 64
14th Congress, 63
investigations of 1965 coup attempt,
14
and military spending in Bulgaria, 12
and political monopoly, 56
and political process, 61
Politburo, 64, 67
Presidium, 64
removal from dominant role, 63
Supreme Party Council, 64
and the Warsaw Pact, 12
and Zhivkov, 62, 66
See also Bulgarian Socialist Party
Bulgarian People's Army (BPA), 14, 55,
99
and civil unrest, 60
and defense policy, 66
defensive sufficiency, 69
and current politics, 70
High Command, 66, 68
1990 political campaign, 65
question of loyalty, 14
and social and political movements,
66–70
Soviet reshaping, 13
See also Anti-Nazi partisans, in the
BPA; Bulgarian Army
Bulgarian Socialist Party (BSP), 66
and coalition building, 65
and elections (1990), 55

headquarters set ablaze in Sofia, 5,
65, 68
name change of BCP to, 64
and 1990 elections, 70
and the "right to rule," 67
Bunic, Simeon, 40
Bush, George, 50, 104

Campeanu, Radu, 76, 80, 82
Carcani, Adil, 22
Carol II, 120
Caucasus, 95, 105
Ceausescu, Elena, 10, 75
Ceausescu, Nicolae, 28, 75, 76, 80, 85
and China, 29(n3)
and cult of personality, 9
demise and execution, 5, 25
and *dezvoltare multilateral,* 10
and human rights, 50
and Mikhail Gorbachev, 10, 11
popularity of, 30(n5)
razing of villages, 12, 27
and Romanian army, 11
and Romanian foreign policy, 9–12
and the USSR, 12, 23
and the Warsaw Pact, 10, 12, 23
Cento, 96
Central Asia, 101
CFE. *See* Conventional Forces in
Europe
Charles XII, 104
Chelac, Sergiu, 75
See also Frontul Salvarii Nationale
China, 50
and Romania, 9, 10
and Southeastern Europe, 7, 8
See also Albania, and China
Christianity
in Southeastern Europe, 2
Chromium, 21
Civil rights
in Bulgaria, 57
CMEA. *See* Council for Mutual
Economic Assistance
Cominform, 16, 21
See also Yugoslavia, expulsion from
Cominform
Communist Party of the Soviet Union
(CPSU), 11
Twenty-first Congress (1961), 17

128   *Index*

Conference for Security and
    Cooperation in Europe (CSCE)
environmental conference in Sofia, 62
and ethnic tolerance, 51
meeting in Stockholm (1985–1986),
    19
Review Conference (1977–1978), 19
Review Conference in Madrid (1980–
    1981), 19
and Southeastern Europe, 27
See also Helsinki Accord
"Consensual economy"
in Yugoslavia, 40
Conventional Forces in Europe (CFE),
    103, 104, 115
Coposu, Cornel, 76
Cordon sanitaire, 16
"Southern Tier," 23, 24
Council for Mutual Economic
    Assistance (CMEA)
and Yugoslavia, 49–50
See also Bulgaria, and the CMEA
Council of Europe's Parliamentary
    Assembly, 57
CPSU. *See* Communist Party of the
    Soviet Union
Croatia, 39
and Agrokomerc, 43
    Croatian crisis (1971), 18
Croatian Democratic Union, 38
Croatian nationalism, 20, 35, 36, 43,
    44
Croatian-Serbian antagonisms, 38
enterprise in, 42
and the JNA, 46
opposition party, 37
police, 39
Protestantism in, 3
reforms in, 5
Roman Catholicism in, 3
and Yugoslav federalism, 46
See also Austro-Hungarian Empire,
    and Croatia
Crowe, William, 96
CSCE. *See* Conference for Security and
    Cooperation in Europe
Cuba, 18
Cunescu, Sergui, 77
Cyprus, 7, 18, 96, 98
Czechoslovakia
invasion of (August, 1968), 8–10,
    21, 24

Dardanelles
Soviet interest in, 24
Delo, 47
Demirel, Suleyman, 92, 93
Democracy
in Central Europe, 120
See also Bulgaria
Democratic Opposition of Slovenia, 38
"Demos." *See* Democratic Opposition
    of Slovenia
Deng, Xiaoping, 21
Dinca, Ion, 75
Dizdareric, Raif, 33(n51), 47
Dnevnik, 47
Dobrudja, 26
Dogovorna ekonomija, 40
Dole, Robert, 98, 114, 115
Dreptatea, 85
Dzhurov, Dobri, 13
and BPA, 67, 68, 70
and the BSP, 69

East Germany
uprisings crushed (1953), 16
Eastern Anatolia, 92, 101
Eastern Mediterranean, 21
EC. *See* European Community
Ecevit, Bulent, 92
Egypt, 50, 115
Emlak Bank scandal, 94
Erbakan, Necmettin, 91
European Community (EC), 50, 94,
    101, 103
Council of Ministers, 113
and economic migration, 3
European integration, 2
and Southeastern Europe, 27
Evren, Kenan, 93
Export-Import Bank, 50

Fischer-Galati, Stephen, 122
Foreign Relations Act of 1960
7:10 ratio, 98
See also Turkey
France, 3, 103, 121
Frontul Salvarii Nationale
and allegations of intimidation, 78
and Ceausescu, 75
and democratic reforms, 80
and discipline in provinces, 86
and electoral procedures, 82

Index

Executive Council, 81
  leadership of, 84
  and the media, 79
  and 1990 elections, 77, 83
  platform, 81
  and popular mandate, 88
  and protests, 76, 85
  role in University Square protests, 86, 87
  and the security establishment, 81
  See also Iliescu, Ion
FSN. *See* Frontul Salvarii Nationale

George II, 120
Germany, 103, 104
  exports to Bulgaria, 72
  "Mitteleuropa," 49
Gheorghiu-Dej, Gheorghe, 9, 30(n5)
Ghitac, Mihai, 81
Giurgiu, 15
Glasnost, 47
Gorbachev, Mikhail
  and the Atlantic-Ural discussions, 104
  and Bulgaria, 56, 61
  and democratization, 33(n54)
  reforms and Turkey, 95
  visit to Yugoslavia, 20
  and Zhivkov, 62, 67, 99, 100
  See also Ceausescu, Nicolae, and Mikhail Gorbachev
Greece, 121
  balance of power with Turkey, 114, 115
  and Bulgaria, 116
  Civil War, 113, 114
  communist insurgences, 97
  debt, 110, 112
  defense policy, 98, 115
  democracy in, 123
  drug issues, 110
  and the EC, 4, 110, 112, 113, 121
  economic reform, 112, 113, 116
  economy, 112
  elections, 109
  ethnics in Albania, 26
  General Confederation of Greek Workers, 113
  inflation, 110, 112, 113
  labor unrest, 113
  Middle East policy, 115
  and NATO, 114, 115

  New Democratic Party, 109–111
  Orthodox Christianity in, 3
  Panhellenic Socialist Movement (PASOK), 97, 109–111
  Parliament. *See* Vouli
  poverty in, 4
  reconciliation with Turkey, 120
  security issues, 115, 116
  socialism in, 111
  social welfare, 113
  and Southeastern Europe, 8
  and Tito, 18
  and Turkey, 7, 26, 97, 99, 102, 104
  and Turkey, Macedonia, 16, 19
  and the U.S., 114, 115
  and the Warsaw Pact, 115
  and Yugoslavia, 26
  See also Ankara Treaty; Balkan Pact; Greek-Bulgarian accord
Greek-Bulgarian Protocol of Friendship and Cooperation (1986), 19, 98
Greek Communist Party (KKE), 109
Gromyko, Andrei, 11

Halikias, Dimitri, 112
Hardt, John, 4
Helinikon Air Base, 98, 114
Helsinki Accord, 19
Helsinki Review Conference, 57
Honecker, Erich, 61
Horvat, Branko, 44
Hoxha, Enver
  and China, 8
  death, 23, 34(n66)
  and nationalist conflicts, 43
Hungary
  and NSWP, 9
  and Romania, 7, 12, 26–28, 78, 86
  and Warsaw Pact, 25
  and Yugoslavia, 51
Hussein, Saddam, 101

Iliescu, Ion, 28
  communist past, 82, 85
  and industrial workers, 86
  and institutional control, 84
  interim presidency, 75
  investigation of miners, 87
  participation in Romanian Communist Party, 84
  political authority, 88

presidential debate, 80
and pro-Front demonstrations, 77
and protests, 76, 86, 123
reliance on industrial labor, 79
and the security establishment, 81
IMF. *See* International Monetary Fund
India, 50
Indonesia, 50
Inonu, Erdal, 93
International Monetary Fund (IMF), 94
and Yugoslavia, 40, 50
Iran, 92, 96
Iraq, 95, 101, 102
Islam
Islamic fundamentalism, 103, 115, 122
Islamic nation, 103
Israel, 115
Istanbul, 4, 91, 100
Italy, 3, 115, 120
fascist Italy and Yugoslavia, 17

Jakes, Milos, 61
Japan, 50
JNA. *See* Yugoslav People's Army
Justice Party, 92

KKE. *See* Greek Communist Party
Khrushchev, Nikita
demise of, 21
removal in October, 1964, 14
"revisionism," 21
and Tito, 16, 17
Knin, 38, 39
Koran, 92
See also Islam
Kos, 115
Kosovo, 3, 26
Albanian nationalist conflict in, 23, 35, 37, 43–46
autonomy of, 38
and the JNA, 49
peace-keeping force deployment, 51
relative well-being in, 48
See also Croatia, Croatian crisis
Krenz, Egon, 61
Kucan, Milan, 38
Kulic, Stavko, 41
Kun, Bela, 119
Kurdish separatism, 4

Kurzhali, 58
Kuwait, 95

LCY. *See* League of Communists of Yugoslavia
League of Communists of Yugoslavia (LCY), 36–38
administration of goods and services, 41
and the Balkans, 20
Central Committee and Kosovo, 45
Central Committee Presidium, 36
and Pristina riots, 44
and USSR, 17
Leninism, 81, 83
Lesbos, 115
Lilov, Alexsandar, 64
and the BPA, 69
and BSP, 67
Little Entente, 120
Ljubljana
economy, 48
and the JNA, 46
Lukanov, Andrei, 63, 64, 102
and the BPA, 69
and BSP, 67
criticism of police, 68

Macedonia, 4, 5, 44, 48
and Albania, 26, 35, 116
economy, 4, 44
nationalists in Greece and Bulgaria, 15
Macedonian nationalism, 27
in Skopje, 19
Mamula, Branko, 20, 45, 46
Mao, Zedong
and Albania, 21
and Romania, 9
Maoism, 21
Markovic, Ante, 36, 39
and debt, 51
and economic reform, 41, 48
emergency measures, 42
and martial law, 44
Mediterranean Sea, 100, 102
Mercin, 104, 115
Mig-25, 49
Mikulic, Branko, 36
and Balkan rapprochement, 19
and Yugoslavian economy, 40

Index

Militaru, General, 80
Milosevic, Slobodan, 3
  criticism of press, 47
  cult of personality, 39
  and martial law, 44
  and the 1974 Constitution, 37
  resistance to economic reform, 41
  rumors of the plot, 46
  and Serbian nationalism, 23, 38, 44,
    45, 49, 51
  and Yugoslav politics, 39
Mitsotakis, Constantine, 97, 109
  campaign, 110, 111
  economic policies, 112, 116
  government, 98, 113, 116
  See also Greece
Mladenov, Petar, 100
  and the BPA, 69
  and the BSP, 67
  and coalition governments, 63
  elevation to Party leadership, 62
  and ethnic Turks, 58
  removal from office, 64
  resignation, 123
Mladina, 47, 53(n23)
Moldavia, 9, 26, 28
Moldova. *See* Moldavia
Montenegro, 5, 44
  economy, 4, 48
  nationalist demonstrations in, 37
  and the JNA, 46
Montreaux Convention, 102
Motherland Party
  elections 1987, 93
  ethnic Turks in Bulgaria, 102
  public support, 94
  and Turkish nationalism, 100
Mutafchiev, General, 65, 68

Narodna Armiya, 14, 45, 65, 69
Nasser, Gamal Abdul, 18, 47, 50
National Peasants Party, 76–77, 78
  See also Coposu, Cornel
National Work Party, 92
NATO. *See* North Atlantic Treaty
  Organization
Nea Makri Air Base, 114
Nehru, Jawaharal, 18, 47, 50
Neo-Stalinism, 21
Nin, 47
Nixon Administration, 113

Nonaligned Movement, 18, 19
  conference in Algiers, 18
  and Yugoslavia, 23, 36, 47, 48, 50,
    51
Non-Soviet Warsaw Pact (NSWP)
  members, 8
  See also Bulgaria, and NSWP;
    Hungary, and NSWP
"Non-Warsaw Pact Autonomous
  Territorial Defense," 25
Non-Warsaw Pact Communist states, 25
"Non-Warsaw Pact Externally
  Dependent Territorial Defense," 25
North Atlantic Treaty Organization
  (NATO)
  and Bulgaria, 66
  and conflicts in Southeastern Europe,
    7
  containment, 96
  and Czechoslovakia and Poland, 50
  and Greek-Bulgarian relations, 98
  Southern Command, 97
  and threats to Turkish security, 102
  and Turkey, 94, 96, 97, 99, 101–103
  Turkey and force levels, 104
  and Turkish-USSR relations, 95
  and Yugoslavia, 49, 50
  See also Greece, and NATO; Turkey,
    and NATO
Northern Epirus, 26
NSWP. *See* Non-Soviet Warsaw Pact
  members

Olteanu, Constantin, 11
Organization for Economic Cooperation
  and Development, 112
Organization of the Islamic Conference
  and Bulgaria, 57
Ostechestven Front, 70
Ottoman Empire, 35, 95, 105, 122
  and Bulgaria, 57
  revolts of 1877, 2
  and Russian intervention, 119
Ozal, Turgut, 122
  and economic deterioration, 94
  1987 election, 93
  and Turkish nationalism, 100
  and Turkish-Soviet relations, 96

Pakistan, 115

Index

Palestine Liberation Organization
(PLO)
and Yugoslavia, 50, 51
Pan Am bombing, 115
Papandreou, Andreas, 122
and Arab relations with the West,
115
and the Greek economy, 110
political decline, 109
and Turkey, 97, 98
and the U.S., 113, 114
"Paracin Massacre," 45
Paris Treaty (1947), 116
Pascu, Ion, 86
PASOK. See Panhellenic Socialist
Movement
Pentagon, 96, 114
Pershing II missile, 114
Persian Gulf War, 95, 101, 102
Philippines, 115
PKK Organization, 101
See also Kuros
PLO. See Palestine Liberation
Organization
Podkrepa, 58, 62, 63
Pomaks. See Bulgaria, Moslems in
Postelnicu, Tudor, 75
Pozderac, Handija, 42
"Prague Spring," 21
Pristina
nationalist conflicts in, 44
riots at University of, 43, 44
suspension of parliament and
government, 44

Rabotnichesko Delo, 99
Radio Free Europe, 30(n10)
Radio Sofia, 64
Rashid, Mohammed, 115
Raskovic, Jovan, 38
Ratiu, Ion, 80, 82
Razgrad
Turkish community in, 58
Reagan, Ronald, 50
Red Army, 96
and Bulgarian Army, 14
in Romania, 9
Roman, Petre, 28, 75
and allegations of intimidations, 77
communist past, 82
and institutional control, 84, 88

and protests, 85
reformism, 81
and the secret police, 87
University Square protests, 85, 87
Romania
Ceausescu, Nicolae. See Ceausescu,
Nicolae
Chamber of Deputies, 84
civil-military relations, 10
Communist Party, 11
and communist rule, 121
Council of National Unity, 82
Defense Council, 11
domestic politics and foreign policy,
9–12
democracy in, 76, 81, 85, 87
ecological movement, 78
economic austerity, 123
economic reform, 88
economy, 79, 81
election monitors, 85
elections of 1990, 5, 78, 82
electoral debate, 80
electoral law, 80
ethnic Hungarians, 77
ethno-nationalism, 78, 79
and human rights, 50
Hungarian Democratic Union, 78, 84
and Hungary, 11, 12
judete, 78
Magyars, 78
media, 79
military exercises, 29(n4)
military expenditures, 11, 31(n15)
militia, 78
miners, 5, 87
Ministry of Internal Affairs, 11
National Assembly, 78
National Liberals, 76–78, 84
National Peasants, 76–78, 84
nationalism, 24
Orthodox Christianity in, 3
Party conference, 1982, 11
radio and television, 79, 80, 86
Red Army control, 97
small-arms industry, 29
Social Democratic Party, 77
Tirgu Mures, 78, 79
University Square protests, 85
and USSR, 9, 26–28
"Vatra Romaneasca," 78

Index

and the Warsaw Pact, 8, 11, 25
and the West, 75, 87
Young Communist League, 84
and Yugoslavia, 51
See also Balkan Pact; Ceausescu,
  Nicolae; Frontul Salvarii Nationale
Romania Libera, 79
Romanian Army, 75, 79, 80
  economic role, 80
  and the University Square protests,
  86
Romanian Communist Party, 81
Ruse
  environmental protests in, 15
Russia, 95
  See also Union of Soviet Socialist
  Republics

Securitate
  and the army, 75
  and ethnic violence, 78
  defeat by army, 50, 86
  and miners, 87
  University Square protests, role in,
  87
  and the urban intelligence, 81
Semerdzhiev, Atanas, 67, 68
Serb, Ion, 10
Serbia, 4, 5, 20, 27, 35–37
  Orthodox Christianity in, 3
  protests in, 41
  reaction to nationalism, 43
  Serb Democratic Party of Knin, 38
  strikes in, 41
  See also Serbian nationalism
Serbian nationalism, 23, 35, 38
  and Albanians, 44
  See also Milosevic, Slobodan
Serbs
  Association of Serbs from Croatia, 38
  in Kosovo, 45
  road blockade by, 39
  See also Croatia, Croatian crisis
Shevardnadze, Eduard, 100
SHP. *See* Social Democrat Populist
  Party
Skopje, 19
Slovenia, 4, 20, 39
  and Agrokomerc, 43
  Albanian minority, 44
  and the Austro-Hungarian Empire, 1

economy, 41, 48
enterprise in, 42
and federal authority, 40
new constitution, 38
opposition party, 37
Protestantism in, 3
reforms in, 5
Roman Catholicism in, 3
Slovene Assembly, 46
Slovene Assembly proclamation of
  sovereignty, 38
Slovene separatism, 35, 43
and Yugoslav federation, 46
Social Democrat Populist Party (SHP),
  93, 94
Sofia
  protests in, 63
Souda Bay
  bases, 98
Souflias, George, 112
Southern TVD. *See* USSR, theatre of
  military operations
Soviet Army
  aircraft, 50
  and Albania, 20
Spain, 115, 120
Stalin, Joseph
  and Cominform, 16
  and the *cordon sanitaire,* 16
  expansionism, 96
  and Tito, 16
  and Yugoslavia, 36
Stanculescu, Victor A., 80, 86
Stefanopoulos, Costas, 110
"Studio Electoral," 80
Suvar, Stipe, 39
Syria, 101

Tanev, Georgi, 68
"Tbilisi," aircraft carrier, 102, 104
Thatcherism, 111
Thrace, 2
Timisoara, 84
Timisoara Proclamation, 82
Tirana
  multilateral diplomatic conference
  (1989), 22
Tito, Josef Broz, 36, 122
  and the Balkan Union, 21
  break from Stalin, 48
  death, 20

and Germany, 49
and nonalignment, 47
Tito's Partisans, 45
"peripatetic summitry," 18
reaction to Croatian nationalism, 43
and Titoism, 16
and the U.S. and West, 17, 49
and the USSR, 8, 17, 18, 23, 24
and Yugoslav communism, 16
and the Yugoslavian economy, 40
See also Greece, and Tito;
  Khrushchev, and Tito; Nonaligned
  Movement; Stalin, and Tito;
  Turkey, and Tito
Titulescu, Nicolae, 119
Todorov-Gorunia, 14
Torumtay, Necip, 96
Transylvania, 26, 30(n6)
and the Austro-Hungarian Empire, 1
protests in, 3
Treaty of Berlin, 2
Treaty of San Stefano, 2
Trenchev, Konstantin, 62, 68
True Path Party, 93
Tsvetkov, Nikolai, 69
Tudjman, Franjo, 38
Turkey, 121
Armenian massacre, 103
balance of payment, 94
and the Balkans, 1
constitution of November, 1982, 92
coup of 1980, 92, 103
democracy, 92–95, 103, 123
domestic policies, 91–95
and the EC, 94, 96, 97, 103, 106
economy, 94
elections of November, 1987, 93
Europeanization, 92, 103
exports, 97
foreign debt, 94, 97
Gulf War military cooperation, 102
human rights issues, 102, 103
inflation, 4, 93, 94
intermediate-range ballistic missiles,
  96
invasion of Cyprus, 96, 98, 103, 115
Islamic fundamentalism in, 91, 92,
  95, 100–102
Mig-25 Fulcrum incident, 96, 104
modernization, 91
Moslems in, 3, 19, 99

National Assembly, 93
Nationals in Bulgaria, 4, 7, 14, 15;
  conscription into BPA, 15
and NATO, 18
Orthodox Christianity in, 3
parliament, 92
population growth in, 3
security issues, 104
and Southeastern Europe, 8
Soviet oil and gas assessment, 102
Soviet trade and business, 102, 106
and Tito, 18
trade deficit, 97
and the U.S., 96, 99, 101, 103, 115
U.S. arms embargo, 96, 98
U.S. bases, 97
and the USSR, 95, 96, 98, 101–103,
  105
visa requirements for Bulgarians, 58
and the West, 91, 92, 94, 95, 102,
  103
See also Ankara Treaty; Balkan Pact;
  Bulgaria, and Turkey; Foreign
  Relations Act of 1960; Greece,
  relations with Turkey; Motherland
  Party
Turkish Communist Party, 92
Turkish Foreign Ministry, 96
Turkish Military, 66, 69, 92
CFE, 104
cooperation with the U.S., 97, 98
political influence, 95
relations with parliament, 92
Turkish general staff, 92, 104
TVD. See USSR, theatre of military
  operations

UDF. See United Democratic Front
UN. See United Nations
Union of Soviet Socialist Republics
  (USSR), 101, 104
arms transfers to Yugoslavia, 49
Chinese threat in Eastern Europe, 7,
  8
economic ties to Yugoslavia, 51
German invasion of, 9
Islamic fundamentalism, 101, 102
and the Nonaligned Movement, 50
Russian Civil War, 119
and Southeastern Europe, 23, 24, 27

theatre of military operations (TVD), 104
Turk-Bulgarian conflicts, 100
Valoma, submarine base, 21
and the Warsaw Pact, 7, 8
western threat in Eastern Europe, 7, 8
withdrawal from Eastern Europe, 20
and Yugoslavia, 20, 24, 29
See also Albania, and the USSR; Balkans, and the USSR; Ceausescu, Nicolae, and the USSR; *Cordon sanitaire*; Tito, and the USSR; Warsaw Pact
United Democratic Front (UDF), 68
and defense, 66, 69, 70
and the 1990 elections, 63–65
United Nations (UN), 27
United States, 94–96, 102
and Balkans, 122
Congress, 4, 98
containment, 96
foreign aid, 114, 115
Libyan conflict, 115
and Nonaligned Movement, 50
press, 85
University Square protests, 85–87
"Declaration" of protestors, 85
Urals, 2
USSR. *See* Union of Soviet Socialist Republics

Valona, Albania, 21
Versailles Conference
Peace Conference, 35
and Southeastern Europe, 49
Vienna
conventional arms talks, 28
Vjesnik, 47
Voican-Voiculescu, Gelu, 76
Vojvodina, 35, 37
autonomy of, 38
Vouli, 109–111

Wallachia, 9
Warsaw Pact, 7, 8
combined armed forces of, 12
and conflict in Southeastern Europe, 7
constraints on military/economic retaliation, 27

"Nominal Warsaw Pact," 25
"Peripheral Warsaw Pact," 25
reorganization of, 24, 25
and Soviet hegemony, 9
"Total Warsaw Pact," 25
Welfare Party, 91, 92
See also Islam; Turkey, Islamic fundamentalism
Western Europe, 103
and diplomatic states of Southeastern Europe, 23
and Yugoslavs, 48
See also Balkans, and Western Europe; European Community
Western Thrace, 98
Wilson, Woodrow
and the Fourteen Points, 35
World War I, 119
World War II, 13
Turkish neutralists, 95
See also Warsaw Pact

Yilmaz, Foreign Minister, 100
Yugoslavia, 5, 121
"all people's defense," 46
Catholicism in, 35
central committee plenum (1988), 39
communists in, 20
Congress (1990), 39
debt, 41, 50, 51
domestic and foreign policy, 16–20
democracy and pluralism in, 47, 48
economic austerity, 123
economy, 49
ethno-nationalism in, 43
expulsion from Cominform (1948), 16, 17, 21
federal presidency, 36, 38
federal system, 47
inflation in, 42
Islam in, 3, 35
labor violence, 41
living standards in, 40
Macedonian issue, 116
martial law (1989–1990), 44
media. *See Borba; Delo; Mladina; Nin; Vejesnik*
Nazi occupation, 36
1974 Constitution, 35, 36, 37
1963 Constitution, 37
Orthodox Christianity in, 35

pluralism, 36, 37
Protestantism in, 35
Republican Central Committee, 42
security in, 18
small-arms industry, 29
Stalinist economy, 40
strikes among miners, 44
study by State Presidency (1987), 37
subsidized living standard, 43
threat of Soviet or NSWP invasion, 26
trade, 50; with Western Europe, 49, 50
and the Warsaw Pact, 8, 16, 25
and the West, 28, 35, 51
and the Yugoslav state, 46
See also Balkan Pact; Bulgaria, and Yugoslavia; Hungary, and Yugoslavia; European Community; Italy, fascist Italy and Yugoslavia; Nonalignment Movement, and Yugoslavia; Palestine Liberation Organization, and Yugoslavia; Romania, and Yugoslavia; Tito, Josef Broz; Union of Soviet Socialist Republics, and Yugoslavia; Western Europe, and Yugoslavs; Wilson, Woodrow, and the Yugoslav state
Yugoslavian army, 17, 38, 40
and civilian unrest, 20
and communist party relations under Tito, 45

and conscripts, 52(n9)
dispatch to Kosovo, 43
Fifth Army Command, 46
and nationalist conflicts, 45, 46
See also "Paracin Massacre"
Yugoslav People's Army (JNA), 39, 44, 45, 46, 49

Zagreb
and the JNA, 46
Zhelev, Zhelyu, 63, 68
presidency, 69
Zhivkov, Todor
arrest, 63
associates, 63
and the BPA, 66
Bulgarian assimilation, 56, 57, 60, 67, 98, 99, 100
and Bulgarian economy, 67
and Bulgarian economic dependency, 13
demise, 62
minority policies, 59
policies against ethnic Turks, 15
reforms, 64
relations with Greece, 15
resignation, 5, 16, 61, 67, 68, 100
rumored plot against, 14
and the Warsaw Pact, 12, 16
See also Bulgaria, and Zhivkov; Gorbachev, and Zhivkov
Zikulov, Vasil, 69
Zog, 120
Zolotas, Xenophon, 110, 113